s.i.m.p.l.i.f.y. your money

DONALD SPILLANE

s.i.m.p.l.i.f.y. your money

First Edition ©2014

ISBN: 0990328309
ISBN 13: 9780990328308

introduction

THERE'S NOTHING SIMPLE ABOUT MONEY AND PERSONAL FINANCES.

"s.i.m.p.l.i.f.y. your money" is an educational process with each letter representing a basic rule designed to help maximize and protect your financial resources. This helps give you increased confidence, and greater feelings of happiness and fulfillment.

Savings: **Take control of your money with less debt and more saving.**

Investments: **Build a safety net before you take on the risk of losing money.**

Mortgages: **Spend a maximum of 25% of gross income on mortgage payments.**

Planning: **You must develop strategies to achieve success in your life's priorities.**

Learning: **Balance college debt against potential career earnings.**

Insurance: **Protect yourself; life doesn't always go the way you plan.**

Fitness: **Like any successful athlete, build reserves to give you strength.**

You: **Take action to achieve your pursuit of happiness.**

"s.i.m.p.l.i.f.y. your money" principles will assist you with understanding basic financial terminology and strategy. This helps you make better informed financial decisions while paying attention to basic common sense.

dedication

This book is dedicated to four of the most important people in my life.
First of all, my mother, Elizabeth, who handled her difficult life with dignity, humor and grace. Second to my sister, Joan, the best sister anybody could have in life, just a peach. Third to my first business mentor, Roz, who gave me such a great start. Last and most to my immensely talented wife, Carol, whose laughter, encouragement, inspiration and love have enriched my life beyond my wildest dreams.

acknowledgements

I'm indebted to a great number of people who have helped me with my financial business and education. I will single out one, Bob Castiliogne, creator of Leap Systems, Inc. His financial model, not a spreadsheet, created from the perspective of an economist, is sheer genius in the way all of any individual's financial decisions can be shown on one piece of paper. His philosophy about money, the way money flows, and its effect on all of us, provides insights into truths that few others even contemplate.

forward

The **"s.i.m.p.l.i.f.y. your money"** guidelines are designed to help you avoid making the same poor financial decisions I made, and I continue to see people making every day. Follow them and they will help you achieve more wealth, confidence, and happiness in your life.

I'm passing on some of my own life experiences for your benefit. Life has treated me well and often, but I also wasted much opportunity by overspending during the good times, and continuing to overspend during the bad times.

It takes a long time to get back on track, and I've reached a better destination by following the guidelines set out in **"s.i.m.p.l.i.f.y. your money."**

We're in an age where reading competes with a host of electronic competitors for our time. At the end of each chapter is the "Chapter Highlights." This is so you can get the essence of the chapter material without all of the detail.

table of contents

chapter one:
s is for savings

TAKE CONTROL OF YOUR MONEY
WITH LESS DEBT AND MORE SAVING.

Chapter One focuses on savings. Descriptions are provided for informational purposes only. Everyone's financial situation is different, and financial purchases should be tailored to the individual. There are no recommendations to purchase products from any particular company. You are strongly advised to consult with experts and licensed professionals, as well as to seek legal and accounting advice, before making your financial decisions.

1. My lifetime income

If you make $75,000 annually for 40 years (aged 25 – 65), your lifetime earnings are $3,000,000. Take away estimated state and federal taxes of 25% and you are left with just over $2,250,000 with which to live, raise a family, buy a house, car, save for retirement, pay college education, vacation, and cover any and all other expenses.

Earnings		$75,000
Taxes	25%	$18,750
Net after Taxes		$56,250
Total time in years	40	
Total Lifetime After Tax Earnings		$2,250,000

Understanding that there is a limit to your lifetime income, that every dollar has to be conserved and planned for, is the first step to understanding and controlling your financial world.

Calculate your lifetime earnings at www.simplifyourmoney.com

2. How much money should I save?

This is an individual decision. Experts recommend different amounts. Your target is to save a minimum of 15% of your annual gross income. Sounds like a lot, doesn't it? It probably is if you're raising a family, but it's not impossible, especially when you have control of your spending and debt.

In the example above, if you saved 15% of your gross income ($937.50 monthly) and could invest it at 4%, after tax, your balance after 40 years would be over $1,100,000.

Income		
Annual Income		$75,000
Monthly Income		$6,250
Taxes	25%	$1,563
Net after Taxes Income		$4,688
Annual Net After Tax Incxome		$56,250
Total employment time in years	40	
Total Lifetime After Tax Earnings		
(Annual Net After Tax Income x Employment Time)		$2,250,000
Savings		
Percentage of Annual Gross Income Saved	15%	$11,250.00
Monthly Savings		$937.50
After Tax Interest Rate	4%	
Total employment time in years	40	
Accumulated Lifetime SavingsValue		$1,108,088.76

a) **Why should I save 15% of my gross income?**

You may not be able to save 15% right away. Work toward this goal by making small adjustments until you get into a comfortable savings mode. Even by saving 15% you will likely have less than 5% true savings over your working life when you consider the following:

- Ever increasing local, state and federal taxes

- Inflation

- Market risk, investment fees and costs

- Interest rate fluctuations

- Raising children and funding their education

- Healthcare costs

- Employment changes

- Legal issues or lawsuits

- Death/Disability/Age (you, family, someone now reliant on you)

- Marriage/Divorce

- Your propensity to spend

- Your propensity to spend your savings

(See further details in Chapter Four: Planning)

3. **When should I start saving?**

- **NOW!**

- Many self-made millionaires live simply, are careful about spending, and avoid debt. Most of them got into the habit of **SAVING** at a young age. Many also worked from a young age at jobs such as paper routes and mowing lawns.

- **The earlier in life you start saving, the greater the amount you can accumulate.**

- For most people, men especially, it's not until relationship and children become a consideration that money management becomes a priority. This can mean missing as much as ten years of savings opportunity. Generally, women seem to be more responsible about their savings.

In Chart 1, Both Man A and Man B each save $2,000 a year. The difference is that Man B didn't start to save until 10 years after Man A had started. By year 40, Man A has $55,000 more dollars saved than Man B.

Chart 1

Years	Man A Amount Saved	Man B Amount Saved	Interest Rate	Man A Cumulative Total	Man B Cumulative Total
1 thru 10	S 2,000.00	S -	3.00%	$22,928	S0
11 thru 20	S 2,000.00	S 2,000.00	3.00%	S53,741	$22,928
21 thru 40	S 2,000.00	S 2,000.00	3.00%	S95,151	S53,741
41 thru 60	S 2,000.00	S 2,000.00	3.00%	S150,803	S95,151

4. Spending

a) How households spends their money[1]

- $21 a week on coffee = $1,092 annually

- $36 a week on lunch = $1,872 annually

- $7 a week on soft drinks= $364 annually

- $500 more a month on lunch and coffee than on commuting costs

- Bottled water is another huge cost. Purchase a filtration system instead.

- Live leaner. Put savings aside and step forward out of the living from paycheck to paycheck mentality.

- You'll feel much better about yourself. Guaranteed.

If you're making $60,000 a year, you should be saving about $25.00 a day.

Huge amounts of you are spending about $10.00 a day on coffee, lunch, and soft drinks.

Cut these discretionary expenses in half and you could save $1,800 in a year, be healthier and happier, and make a big dent in the $25 daily goal.

---

[1] **Workonomix survey 2012 and 2013 by finance recruiting firm Accounting Principles.**

b) Our priorities are in the wrong order

Between 2010 and 2011, spending on personal insurance and pension contributions remained almost the same, while spending on entertainment and food rose 5.4%.

Salaries rose by 1.9% during the same period. If you received a pay increase, what did you do with it? Spend or save? Make sensible decisions.

Item	2010	2011	2010-2011 Change
Average Income (before tax)	$ 62,481	$ 63,685	1.90%
Food	$6,129	$6,458	5.40%
Housing	$16,557	$16,803	1.50%
Apparel and Service	$1,700	$1,740	2.40%
Transportation	$7,677	$8,293	8.00%
Healthcare	$3,157	$3,313	4.90%
Entertainment	$2,504	$2,572	5.40%
Cash Contributions	$1,633	$1,721	5.40%
Personal Insurance and Pensions	$5,373	$5,424	0.90%

A partial table taken from a Bureau of Labor Statistics press release September 25, 2012

c) The good news

You can change your life if you take the money you are wasting and put it to good use. You'll save money if you avoid **overindulging** on food and entertainment. Add in excessive spending on the kids, and there's the difference between being broke and in debt, to saving money.

d) The bad news

You have to change your lifestyle. Change is something most people find very challenging as it requires effort when it's easier to accept staying in the same place. However, it's the only way forward when you have wasteful spending habits, are in debt up to your eyeballs, have little long-term savings, inadequate insurance of all types, no protection against a sudden expense, live paycheck to paycheck, and pretend to be happy.

e) Teamwork

For the married and the living together, financial stress is the root cause of most problems and often leads to divorce and separation. You can remove many of these problems through communication, forgiveness, and understanding. These are powerful tools when you're trying to solve your joint money problems. Teamwork will help you cope with family financial decisions:

- Family life puts enormous pressure on your finances.

- The peer pressure on your children to fit in to their social scene can be a huge financial drain on your resources. Purchases of cell phones, computers, video games, clothing, internet and phone service costs, and other expenses, add up quickly.

- **It's not a stretch to say, "If you give it all to your children now, they may end up supporting you in your old age."**

- There are many hard choices to make, and you'll probably need help.

- You might even know what you have to do, but lack the discipline and attitude to get it done.

5. Five steps to success in saving

Step 1: Keep thorough financial records

You need to know in detail how much money is earned versus how much money is spent.

- Begin now.

- Keep records.

- Record everything, EVERYTHING, you spend AT THE TIME.

- Check your bank account before shopping. Know your limits.

- Plan your purchases ahead of time to **avoid impulse buying.**

- Take a photo of the price tag from your phone. Use a mobile app to track spending.

- Knowing you will go through these steps, will often make you question your purchase.

- Keeping track of your spending allows you to see where you can save.

- **Use cash as much as possible**. Using a debit or credit card doesn't give money the same value as spending actual cash.

- You may qualify to save on medical expenses through a tax-free program such as a Flexible Spending Account (FSA), or a Wellness program. (See Chapter Six: Insurance.)

- Save money on transportation and parking costs by registering your company's pre-tax program allowing you $250 per month for parking and $130 for commuter costs. Commuting by bicycle can generate $20 monthly in non-taxable income, as well as deductions for the cost of the bicycle and reasonable repairs. [2]

A dollar here and a dollar there seems insignificant, but not when it means you're controlling your money instead of it controlling you. Paying attention to the little things is half of the battle. This is a lifestyle change that will benefit you enormously.

_____

[2] Source: http://www.irs.gov/pub/irs-pdf/p15b.pdf

Step 2: Organize your financial records into a system

Whatever record-keeping method you use, it's very important that you be able to find any record quickly and easily. There are good off-the-shelf programs to help you get organized such as Quicken, Excel, any spreadsheet program or app, or even hanging files in a cabinet.

Whatever system you choose, it must be organized. Group your files in clusters for convenience and ease of use. It's helpful to use a different color to differentiate each group.

- One group could be savings: both short and long term for education, tax-free and tax-deferred accounts.

- Another might be all insurance policies: car, home, umbrella, health, life and disability, and employment insurance benefits A third group would be investments: bonds, stocks, real estate, and collectibles

- Include files for your wills and/or trusts, along with the life insurance policies.

Step 3: The monthly household budget

The purpose of this account is to allow you to see how you are spending your money, and allocate an amount that will cover your monthly expenses. The amount will vary depending on your circumstances. Transportation costs, utility bills, and other expenses may vary each month.

Print out your own monthly budget sheet below at: www.simplifyourmoney.com

Monthly Take Home Pay			Contributions to Savings	
Spouse/Partner	S		Emergency Savings	S
Spouse/Partner 2	S		Savings Accounts	S
Bonus/Commission	S		401(k)	S
Income from Inheritance	S		Roth IRA	S
Royalties	S		Investment Account	S
Rental Income	S		Other	S
Additional Income	S		Other	S
Other Income	S			
Total Monthly Take Home Income	$		**Total Monthly Savings**	$
Monthly Income left after Savings	$		**Savings as a Percentage of Monthly Income**	

Monthly Expenses				
Housing			**Auto**	
Mortgage / Rent	S		1st Car payment	S
2nd Mortgage	S		2nd Car Payment	S
Real Estate Taxes	S		3rd Car Payment	S
Home/Renter's Insurance	S		Car Insurance	S
Association Fees	S		Gas	S
Repairs/Maintenance	S		Service	S
Credit Line	S		Repairs/Tires/Brakes	S
Other	S		License/Taxes	S
Other	S		Parking	S
	S		Toll Fees	S
	S		Other	S
Housing Expense Total	$		**Auto Expense Total**	$

Household Expenses			Consumer Debt Payments	
Oil	S		Visa 1	S
Gas	S		Visa 2	S
Water	S		MasterCard 1	S
Electricity	S		MasterCard 2	S
Trash	S		American Express	S
Cable	S		Discover	S
Internet	S		Retail Store Card 1	S
Phone	S		Retail Store Card 2	S
Phone/internet/Cable	S		Discover	S
Cleaning / Laundry	S		Bank Loan	S
Cell 1	S		Student Loan 1	S
Cell 2	S		Student Loan 2	S
Cell 3	S		Student Loan 3	S
Gardner	S		Other	S
Pool	S		Other	S
Groceries	S		**Consumer Debt Total**	$
Pet Food	S			
School Supplies	S		**Medical Expenses**	
Childcare/Babysitting	S		Health Insurance	
Gym Membership	S		Co-Pays	
Hair/Manicure	S		Prescriptions	
Cosmetics	S		FSA Contributions	
Vacation	S		Other	
Entertainment	S		Other	
Gifts/Charity	S			
School Fees	S		**Medical Expense Total**	$
Life Insurance 1	S			
Life Insurance 2	S			
Disability Insurance	S		**Total Monthly Income**	$
Liability Insurance	S		**Less Monthly Savings**	$
			Less Household Budget	$
Household Expense Total	$		**Balance Owed / Over**	$
Household Budget = Housing Expense plus Household Expense plus Consumer Debt plus Medical Expenses				

Your household budget is a sum of the following expense totals:

- Housing Expenses
- Household Bills
- Auto Expenses
- Consumer Debt
- Medical Expenses

Step 4: Bank accounts

a) The Prosperity Account

You will do best with two bank accounts. Name the first, The Prosperity Account, or something similar.

This account is used for channeling your money into various savings, retirement, and investments vehicles.

- Make all deposits, including salary checks, into the Prosperity Account.
- Be sure to account for retirement contributions deducted from your pay automatically, such as your 401(k) contribution. These count toward the 15% goal and won't show in this account. Cash-value life insurance payments also count toward the 15% savings goal.

b) The Household Account

This is an account used to pay the items in your household budget.

- Electronically send the amount detailed by your Household Budget to your Household Account from your Prosperity Account.
- Work toward a **goal** of having at least 15% of your gross income left in the Prosperity Account, after transferring the Household Budget.
- Preferably, it should be a very low or no-fee account, allowing you to electronically draft through online banking.
- Electronically pay your bills from this account according to your Household Budget.
- Online banking offers the biggest savings in time and convenience.

If you're broke, set goals and work toward them by becoming more frugal. Money going out is not sustainable if it exceeds money coming in. Continuing on a path of debt to maintain a lifestyle, increases your financial woes and stress, and is simply not sustainable.

When the government spends more than it takes in, it just prints more money. You can't. Even for the government, this is not sustainable in the long term.

Step 5: Monitoring and adjusting

Your reformed financial habits now include the vital task of monitoring your savings and expenditures no less than monthly.

- Your gains may be very small, but use any money saved to reduce debt and/or to add to your savings and protection areas.
- Always balance your bank accounts.

Add any of the following to your Prosperity Account:

- Salary Increases
- Tax Refunds
- Bonuses
- Any new money that comes your way such as an inheritance.

6. Helpful hints

Many of the following items are already known to you. **Taking action is the key to success.**

- You probably qualify to save on medical expenses through a tax-free program like Flexible Spending Account (FSA). (See Chapter Six: Insurance)
- Save money on health insurance through a Wellness program. (See Chapter Six: Insurance)
- Consumer debt interest, (auto, credit cards etc) is not tax deductible, but loans secured by real estate offer tax deductions on the mortgage interest. Consolidate consumer loans into a home equity line of credit, and obtain a tax deduction on the interest.
- Don't forget the home office deduction when you work from home and have space set aside as an office.
- Where practical, raise the deductibles on your auto and homeowners insurance to save money on your premium. (See the Chapter Six: Insurance)
- Save money by registering for a tax-free program allowing you $130 monthly for commuter transportation, and $250 monthly for parking costs.
- Using your bicycle for commuting can also offer tax savings.
- Save money through using carpools and public transportation.
- Plan to keep alternative fuel and hybrid autos for longer than five years to be cost effective.
- Read magazine and newspapers online. Avoid paying a subscription.
- Be aware of automatic renewals as a default, especially with online orders.
- Use coupons where practical and possible.

- Budget your cable and satellite bills sparingly. Even with 500 channels available, is there anything on that's worth the cost to your savings?

- Shopping online provides a good way to compare your costs and find the best price for purchases.

- Electronic banking is efficient, and can offer competitive rates and terms. Online banks don't have the overhead expense of a conventional brick and mortar bank.

a) Should I buy or lease my car?

When you purchase a car you pay for the whole vehicle. This means coming up with a down payment and financing the balance over a term of years. Generally, a longer term earns a higher interest rate. You also have to pay sales tax and licensing fees that are often rolled into your overall loan.

When you lease a car, you are paying for the use of the car. There is usually very little down payment. Sales tax and licensing fees can be rolled into the monthly lease payment. One big issue on leasing is mileage limitation which is generally 12,000 miles annually. The penalty for exceeding the mileage lit is usually 15 cents per mile.

Generally, over a 6 year period (two 3 year lease terms), it is more expensive to lease a new car versus buying either a new or used car. The difference is that you have driven a new car for 2 three years periods as opposed to having a six year old car if you bought new or even older if you bought used.[3]

7. Goals and rewards

Setting goals is very important. This allows you to compare where you are today alongside where you want to be in several year's time. Just as important, it shows you how far you've come. Examining how much you've progressed on life's voyage will lift your spirits. Look at what you've achieved in the past. It tells you what you CAN do.

- Break larger goals down into smaller, more manageable steps.

- Achieving each step leads you toward your goal.

- Decide on a small reward as you achieve each step.

- Getting started and procrastination are always big problems. Get some help from a coach, friend, or financial planner. (See more in Chapter 4: Planning)

8. Dealing with debt

Getting into debt is far easier than getting out of debt. We live in a world where we're encouraged to take on more debt to enjoy our lives with something we just can't live without. We're bombarded 24/7 with unwanted advertisements along with media coverage of the latest and greatest.

---

[3] http://www.edmunds.com

- Pay your bills as they arrive and don't delay payment until the due date.

- This process will help keep your credit intact, and avoid late payments by mistake.

- Using an automatic debit is an efficient way to pay bills, save time, and even earn discounts from retailers.

a) Solve debt problems by monitoring expenditures

One of the biggest keys to solving excessive debt is monitoring expenditures. This comes back to budgeting and tracking discretionary spending, and cash purchases.

b) Which debt should I pay off first?

Concentrate on paying off the highest interest rated debt first. It's probably a credit card. Once you pay it off, select your next highest interest rate loan, and concentrate your efforts there.

- Some people subscribe to the theory that it's best to pay off smaller loans first and not worry about the interest rate. It's true that paying off a couple of smaller debts with lower interest rates gives you quick victories, and a feeling of moving forward.

- It may not be the best option mathematically, but any victory will make you feel good and help encourage you to take on bigger challenges.

- As you pay off each loan balance, the monthly payment is freed up. Use it as payment on the next loan you target to pay off, or use it to build up your financial security.

- Don't spend the payment savings!

c) I can't pay my debt

The biggest reasons given for having overwhelming debts are:

- Sickness and medical bills

- Loss of job

- Divorce

- Unable to control excessive spending

Solutions include:

- Having a safety net to help soften the blow

- Payment agreements with lenders and collections agencies

- Credit counseling

- Bankruptcy: Chapters 11, 13, and 7

- Follow the **s.i.m.p.l.i.f.y.** philosophy to help you build your safety net.

d) Dealing with lenders and collection agencies

Many lenders and collections agencies alienate themselves by being emotionally remote in their communications. Most letters are computer generated. You're just another number in the line and you're made to feel that way. It's hard not to be frustrated and angry when dealing with debt problems, especially when you have others dependent on you for support.

- It's essential that you calm your emotions and negotiate a payment agreement that you can afford.

- Work as a team if you're a couple.

- The willingness to pay something goes a long way with creditors. They'd rather see you pay the debt over time, than have to go through the expense of a judgment to recover the amount owed.

- Keep your agreements.

- It pays to communicate with debtors and tell them what you can do, rather than just ignoring them and aggravating an already bad situation.

- Know your rights. There are state laws and regulations, which govern the collection of debt to prevent harassment.

e) Credit counseling

A credit counseling company negotiates with the lender to come up with a workable plan to pay off your loans. A good credit counselor can be helpful, but be aware that the industry's reputation is one of poor credibility and excessive costs.

- Do your research.

- Ask your professional advisors and friends for recommendations of reputable companies.

9. Bankruptcy

Bankruptcy may be the best option and it doesn't necessarily mean you cannot get credit at all. It means that any credit you get will be at a very high interest rate.

- Always consult with a certified public accountant, (CPA), and a bankruptcy attorney, to consider all of your options. The most frequently used forms of bankruptcy are known as Chapters:

a) Chapter 7

Assets are liquidated by the bankruptcy trustee for the benefit of creditors.

b) Chapter 11

A reorganization and repayment plan for businesses. Unlike Chapter 13 there is no debt limitation for filers.

c) Chapter 13

A court-supervised repayment plan, which protects you against further attempts to collect on the debt. At the end of the plan all debts are discharged.

10. Waiting periods for bad credit

Be aware that a poor credit history, (derogatory events) has a significant impact on your borrowing power, and the interest rate on loans, especially mortgages. When applying for a mortgage, you may have to wait before applying for a loan. Here are some of the criteria that obtaining the loan may be dependent upon:

- The lender

- Any extenuating circumstances

- The type of poor credit on the report

- Your FICO score

- For example, a Chapter 7 or Chapter 11 bankruptcy, under a Fannie Mae insured loan, means you may have to wait as long as four years, whereas with an FHA loan you may only have to wait two years.

- Lenders will also be looking for a stable income, low debt to income ratio, and an adequate down payment. For more information see Chapter Three: Mortgages.

11. Chapter One: Highlights

- What is your lifetime income? $75,000 annually from age 25 through 65 gives you a lifetime income of $3,000,000. Before taxes. For everything you do in life. Not so much now, is it?

- Understanding there is a limit to your income, and every dollar has to be conserved, planned for, and used efficiently, is the first step to understanding and controlling your financial world.

- Target 15% of gross income for savings to counter the effects of increases in taxation, inflation, interest rate fluctuations, and loss of employment.

- You should start saving now! The earlier in life you start saving, the greater the amount you accumulate.

- The first place to look for savings opportunities is your discretionary spending. Many people are spending over $1,000 a year just buying coffee.

- You may have to change your lifestyle, which is difficult but very important, when you know you are in a death spiral as far as your money is concerned.

- Family life puts a huge pressure on finances. Avoid overindulging either yourself, or especially your children. The peer pressure on children to have the latest cell phone, video game, or sneakers is tremendous, but these expenditures should always fit in your budget.

- If you give it all to your children now, they may end up supporting you in your old age.

- Avoid feeling entitled to make purchases just because you work hard.

- Use cash where possible. Credit and debit cards make spending too easy.

- Married couples and partners can avoid conflict by working together on their financial plans.

- Work toward having a minimum of six months cash savings available for emergencies.

- Keep thorough and accurate financial records. Record everything you spend, especially cash.

- Plan purchases ahead of time to avoid impulse buying.

- Control your money, instead of allowing it to control you.

- Organize financial records into a physical or electronic file. Group similar subjects together. Insurance policies, mortgage statements, bank information, retirement account statements, and investment accounts should be separated and filed accordingly.

- Open a bank account as your Prosperity Account. All deposits go here first. Draft to your various investment and long term savings accounts from here.

- Have another account for your Household Budget. This account will contain Housing expenses, household bills, car expenses, debt payments and medical expenses.

- Electronically draft your Household Budget from your Prosperity Account.

- In an ideal situation, after drafting your household expenses, the prosperity account will contain at least 15% of your gross paycheck. Work toward this goal.

- Monitor financial affairs no less than monthly.

- Salary increases, tax refunds, bonuses, and any other new money, such as an inheritance should be added to your prosperity account.

- Set targets and know what small rewards you will give yourself when you achieve them. Take time to smell the roses.

- Take advantage of tax-free medical savings plans like an FSA. Wellness plans also offer the opportunity to save on medical costs.

- Where practical, save on your auto insurance by raising your deductible to an acceptable limit. (See Chapter Six: Insurance)

- Don't forget the company offered pre-tax savings plans of $130 monthly for commuting costs, as well as $250 monthly for parking fees.

- Budget cable and satellite costs sparingly. Do you really need 500 channels when you probably can't find anything decent to watch anyway?

- Plan to keep alternative fuel and hybrid autos for at least five years for them to be cost effective.

- Shop online to easily compare costs and get the best deals. Online retailers do not have the expense of a brick and mortar store.

- Pay all your loan payments as they are presented to you. That will help improve and maintain your on-time payment record.

- Solve debt problems by first of all monitoring spending.

- Mathematically, it's better to pay off the higher interest rate credit debt first. However, it's also about feeling like you're making progress, so paying off a smaller balance, which has a lower interest rate, gives you that all important emotional lift.

- When you pay off a debt do not spend the payment saving. Either save it, or put it toward the next debt.

- Solutions to being unable to pay debt include: having a safety net to soften the blow, payment agreements with lenders, credit counseling, and bankruptcy.

- A poor payment record can remain on your credit report for years. When applying for a mortgage, you may have to wait before applying for a loan depending on the lender, whether or not there are extenuating circumstances, the type of the report, and your FICO score. For example, with Chapter 7 or 11 bankruptcies; under a Fannie Mae insured loan you may have to wait as long as four years, whereas with an FHA loan you may only have to wait two years.

- Above all, BE PATIENT. Don't beat yourself up should you lapse into old habits. Take a breath and keep moving forward. Minor changes can make a big difference to both your purse and confidence.

- **Taking action is the key to success.** (See Chapter Eight: You)

- Over time, as your financial picture improves, a cushion of liquid reserves and protection for you and your family will increase your confidence.

chapter two:
i is for investments

Chapter Two focuses on investments. Descriptions are provided for informational purposes only. Everyone's financial situation is different, and financial purchases should be tailored to the individual. There are no recommendations to purchase products from any particular company. You are strongly advised to consult with experts and licensed professionals, as well as to seek legal and accounting advice, before making your financial decisions.

1. Growing wealth without a safety net

Many people make the mistake of starting their first financial steps, by attempting to grow their wealth quickly, using the stock and real estate markets. This is where you can lose some, or all, of your money.

For a precious few, growing wealth as quickly as possible, and taking on risk without a safety net works. For the vast majority, it's a losing strategy where substantial risk without a safety net is a contributing cause to financial failure.

Further proof that you need a safety net before investing:

Measures of Household Wealth

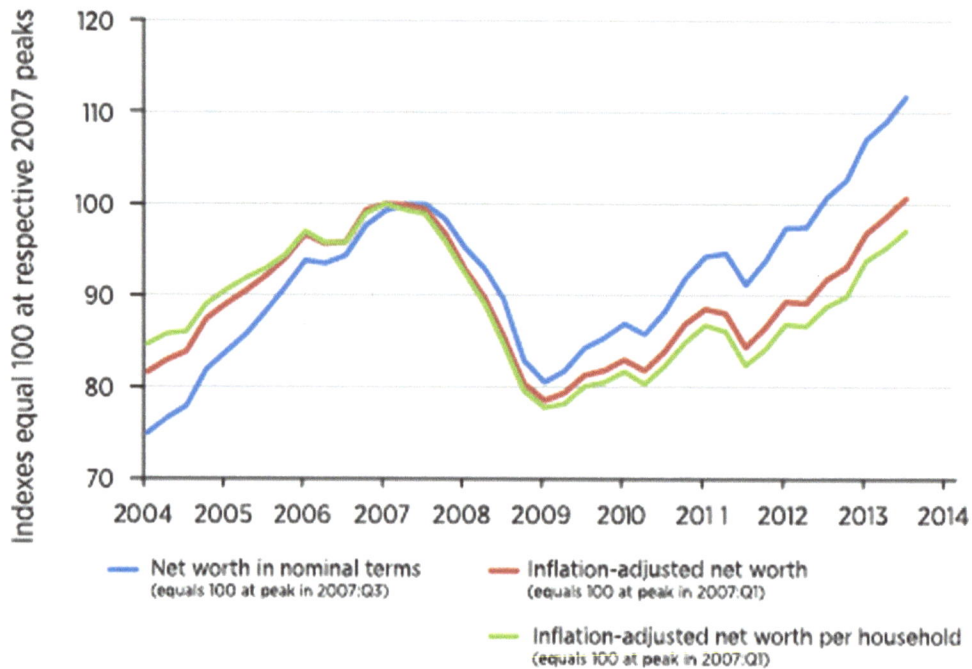

This graph shows a peak in 2007 to a low point in the first quarter of 2009 during the recession. Since 2009[4]:

- When measured through the third quarter of 2013 and with inflation factored in, the average household has still not regained the wealth lost in 2007.

- Wealthier families, more able to afford the risk, have made stronger gains mainly through the stock market.

- For younger, less educated, and lower-income families, home values represent the largest part of their wealth.

- The economically vulnerable, often with over-financed housing, are left with little margin for error.

2. What is my safety net?

A safety net exists when you've taken care of basic financial risk to yourself and /or your family, by putting safeguards in place should an unforeseen event occur. Most people, especially the young, ignore having these safeguards in place at their financial peril. Being prepared is your best defense, whether you are young, middle-aged, or old.
Your safety net should include the following:

- A bank account with adequate liquid cash reserves.

---

[4]   Federal reserve Board, Bureau of Economic Analysis, , published May, 2013

- Adequate liability protection against lawsuit from accident and events.
- Protection against disability and death.
- Protection against short and long-term illness, including hospitalization.
- Protection for your retirement account should you not be able to work.
- Having up-to-date wills and trusts, with correct beneficiaries in place.

3. Why should I invest?

Liquid or cash savings provide limited, if any, protection against inflation. Current interest rates on most savings accounts are extremely low. Gains are being eaten away by inflation levels as well as increased taxation.

Investing, while providing more risk, provides the opportunity to obtain a bigger return on your money, and hopefully outpace the rate of inflation.

4. How does corruption and market risk affect my money?

Your wealth is threatened by two unpredictable factors:

a) **The market risk with the investments you make.**

b) **Corruption and fraud within the system.**

- Both can lead to substantial losses, especially to your retirement account.
- You have zero control.
- Employees lose jobs, retirement money, and stock options.
- Investors lose money.
- Top management seems to survive intact with big pension payouts and golden parachutes.

As an individual, you will continue to have little influence either on the market, or the political world. Your vote might offer influence, but the politicians are making the laws and conducting investigations while making little headway with enforcement.

For many companies, paying fines without admitting responsibility or liability, are the costs of doing business.

5. Combine investments to meet overall objectives

Balance the risk in your investments with your safety net firmly in place to cover any weaknesses.

- Don't try to build a financial castle without a foundation.
- Purchase products that meet your personal, professional, and financial priorities. (See Chapter Four: Planning)

a) Asset allocation

This is an investment strategy to minimize risk and maximize gain by investing your portfolio among different asset classes such as stocks, bonds, and cash equivalents.

- Financial goals, time of life, and your risk tolerance become important in creating the right mix of assets. For example, if you're near retirement you might be less inclined to take on a high-risk strategy.

- Creating the balance between risk and return is difficult, and will obviously have a major impact on the achievement of your financial goals.

b) Asset diversification

This is an investment strategy to reduce risk by spreading investments over both a number of different asset classes, and within those classes. For example:

- Stocks: large, small, and international companies

- Bonds: tax free, municipal, long term

- Cash equivalents: treasury bills, government savings bonds, certificates of deposit

6. The investor's emotional rollercoaster [5]

Markets generally are driven by emotions, especially fear and greed: fear of loss and fear of being left out of something good combined with greed to get as much as possible. These are the extremes, but emotions play a large part in our decision-making, and the following diagram illustrates how emotions are reflected in the varying fortunes of a market. These emotional buttons are continually punched by the headline-seeking media.

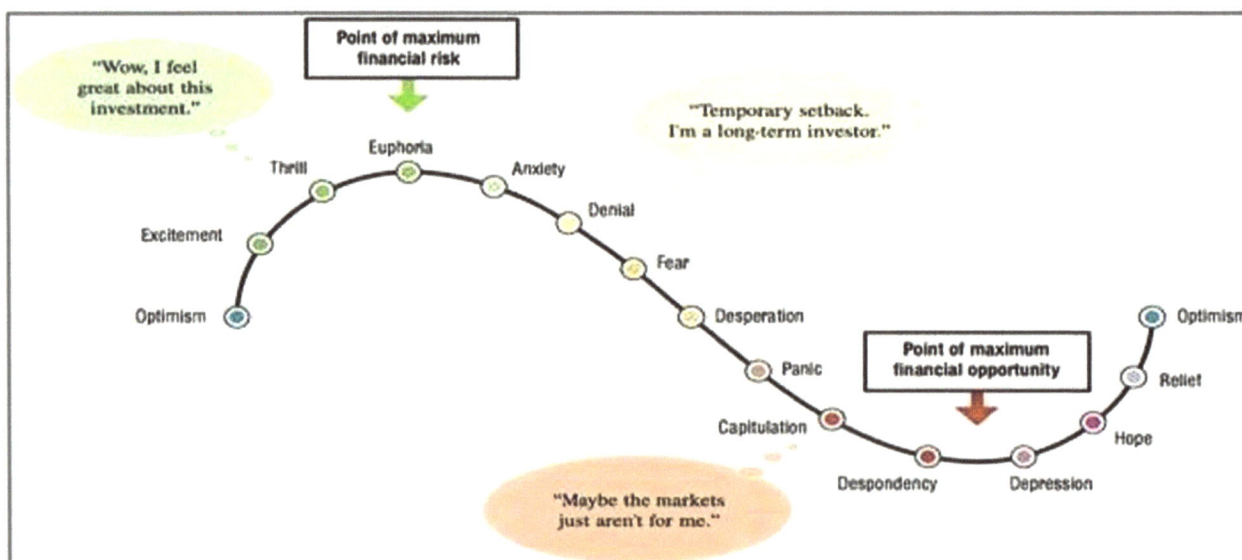

---

[5] Source: optionalpha.com

7. Bonds

A bond is a loan. Buying a bond means you have loaned your money to a company, state, or to the US federal government. There are a number of different types of bonds offering various levels of return and conditions. Generally:

- You receive income and cash flow as the loan and interest is repaid.

- Bonds, some tax free, are purchased and used for generating income.

- The loan is for a set period of time at a stated interest rate, mostly fixed for the life of the bond.

- The return on a bond varies according to interest rates. A bond's value decreases when interest rates rise and increases as rates fall. Something to consider in this low interest environment.

- Bonds are not as volatile as stocks and are purchased on a long-term basis with fairly predictable results.

- Bonds can be purchased by their maturity date, the issuer, their quality, and by tax status.

- There is a risk of default. The threat that Detroit, and other cities, will default on their bond and pension fund obligations is very real, particularly with bankruptcy being an option.

- The bond market is not immune to fraud, with recent investigations of a number of municipalities for "material omission" and "false statements" in their municipal bond offerings.[6]

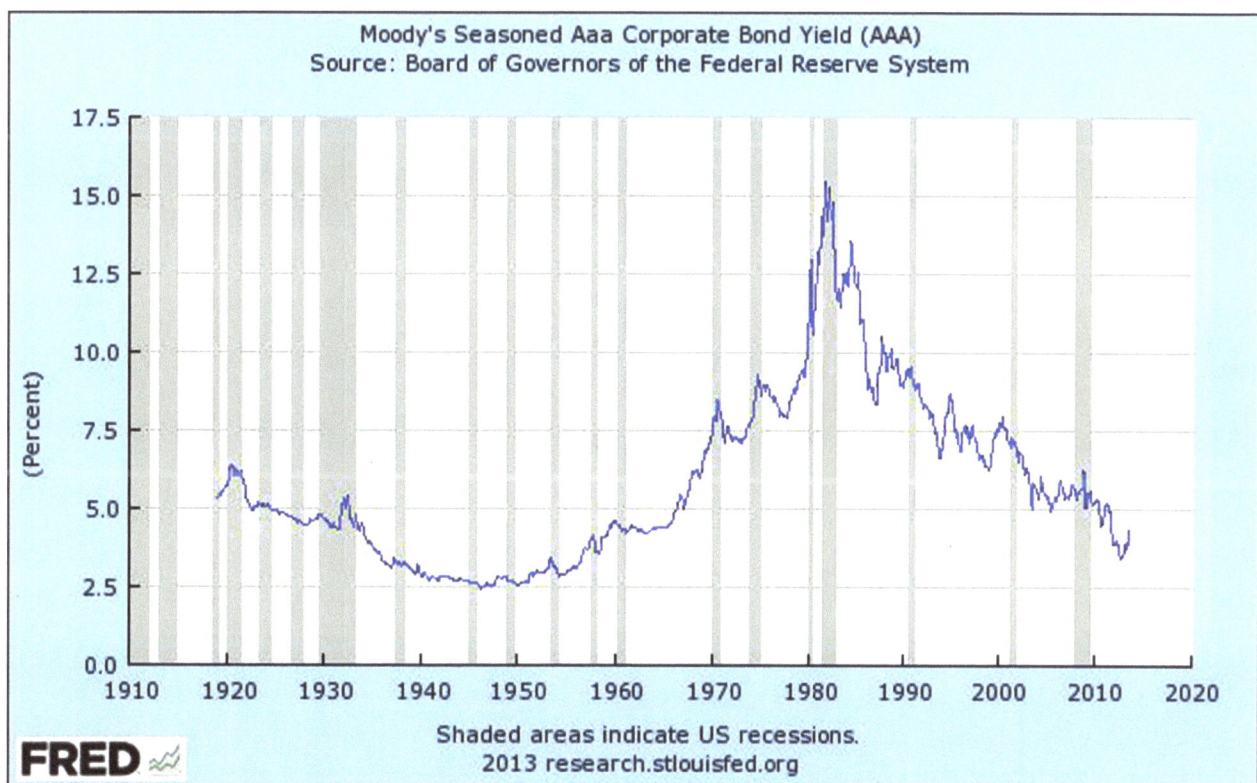

Moody's Seasoned Aaa Corporate Bond Yield (AAA)
Source: Board of Governors of the Federal Reserve System

Shaded areas indicate US recessions.
2013 research.stlouisfed.org

FRED

---

[6] Steve Malanga, Wall St. Journal, "The Many Ways That Cities Cook Their Books." 6-1-2013

8. Stocks and shares

Stocks and shares are the same thing, with each term used according to context. They are purchased to grow wealth and/or generate income. You are making an investment in a company by purchasing a share of the company. (See Paragraph 6 above relating to the emotional rollercoaster)

- 2012/2014 has seen an increase in stock market prices. Volatility and uncertainty remain a problem. It remains to be seen what the future holds for the economy in which seems there seems to be little confidence from the American public.

- As stated above, with inflation factored in, the average household has regained only half of the wealth it lost earlier in the decade.

The following graph shows the big picture of stock market trends from 1900 through 2009. It's worth noting that periods of growth last about 20 years, and these are followed by a leveling-off in growth for similarly long periods.[7]

Dow Jones Historical Trends

History shows that the market typically moves in cycles. In the past 113 years, there have been four bull markets (shown in blue) and four bear markets (shown in red) Investment strategies that work in bull markets may not be effective in flat or bear markets.

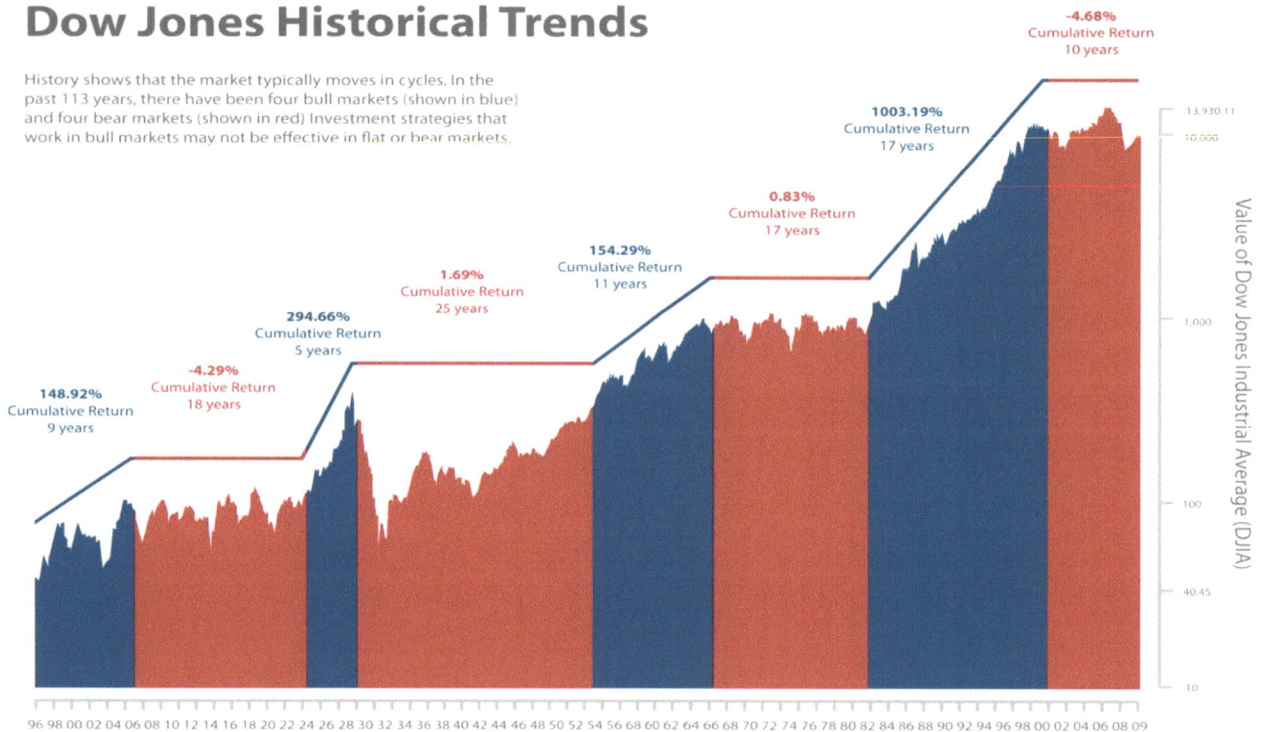

-4.68%
Cumulative Return
10 years

1003.19%
Cumulative Return
17 years

0.83%
Cumulative Return
17 years

154.29%
Cumulative Return
11 years

1.69%
Cumulative Return
25 years

294.66%
Cumulative Return
5 years

-4.29%
Cumulative Return
18 years

148.92%
Cumulative Return
9 years

Value of Dow Jones Industrial Average (DJIA)

13,930.11
10,000
1,000
100
40.45
10

96 98 00 02 04 06 08 10 12 14 16 18 20 22 24 26 28 30 32 34 36 38 40 42 44 46 48 50 52 54 56 68 60 62 64 66 68 70 72 74 76 78 80 82 84 86 88 90 92 94 96 98 00 02 04 06 08 09

Logarithmic graph of the Dow Jones Industrial Average from 12/1896 through 12/2009.
Source: Graph created using data from www.dowjones.com01/2010.
Performance display represents past performance, which is no guarantee of future results. The Dow Jones Industrial Average is unmanaged and unavailable for direct investment. Returns do not reflect any dividends, management fees, transaction costs or expenses.

---

[7] Source: advadisor.wordpress.com

There are two kinds of stocks:

a) Common stock

Common stocks are volatile with high risk attached. As we have seen over the past ten years, there can be wild fluctuations in the markets. Huge gains one day followed by huge losses the next, with heavy media coverage of the rollercoaster ride.

b) Preferred stock

Shareholders receive earnings before the common stock owner, and have first choice on company assets in the event the company is liquidated.

- Company profits are distributed to preferred stockholders using dividends.
- Preferred stocks generally offer a better yield and less volatility than common stock.
- Blue chip stock, refers to stock purchased in well-established companies that are likely to pay dividends in both good and bad economic times.

The stock markets have enjoyed significant growth during 2011/2014. Much of this growth can be attributed to the low interest rates providing a poor return for savers. People are encouraged to invest because inflation has eaten away any growth offered at lower interest rates. The question is always, "How sustainable are the gains?"

9. Mutual funds

A mutual fund is a way of investing by pooling your money with a group of other investors to purchase stocks, bonds, real estate, or other securities. This offers diversity. They are often linked to a benchmark index, for example, S&P 500. There are thousands of funds to choose from. They fall into two types:

Actively managed funds: A fund manager is employed to buy and sell with the objective of beating the performance of a benchmark index. From June 1998 through June 2013, only 25.6% of funds managed to beat their benchmark index, yet the fees and expenses are higher than passively managed funds.[8]

Passively managed funds: A fund manager tries to match the performance of the index by purchasing only securities within that index.

- Mutual Funds provide diversification because they allow the purchase of a broad range of investments that an individual investor would otherwise find unaffordable.
- Each fund provides a different way of investing, although the largest focus is on stocks.
- 93% of people who own mutual funds do so with retirement as their main objective[9].
- The funds are professionally managed, meaning that you typically pay fees, although passively managed funds offer lower expenses.
- Shareholders share losses and gains proportionately.

[8] Source: Gerstein Fisher, In Mutual Funds, is Active vs. Passive, the Right Questions? Summer 2013

[9] Source: Investment Company Institute, Company Fact Book 2013, "Characteristics of Mutual Fund Investors," Figure 6.2

- Fund shares can be bought and sold on the same day offering liquidity.

- Your investment is not guaranteed by the federal government, and you risk losing some or all of your investment.

- You should anticipate annual capital gains and tax on dividends at the local, state, and federal level. If you are investing through a tax-advantage program, such as retirement accounts, the taxes will be deferred.

- According to an article in Moneylife, "Why people lose money in mutual funds." The reason investors lose money in mutual funds is that they put their money into equity mutual funds at the wrong time, when the market is highly valued. They become disappointed and then sell when the market is down.[10]

a) Fees

A mutual fund prospectus will define the fees and charges directly imposed on you at the time of the transaction under the heading, "Shareholder Fees." Other investor paid fees are listed under "Annual Fund Operating Expenses." Calculating the actual fees you pay is often very difficult. It can depend on the type of share within the fund, and whether you use the services of a professional.

I. Shareholder fees include:

- *Load:* A sales charge, or commission, paid by investors to the selling brokers. Some funds not using outside brokers still charge a fee. These are not permitted to exceed 8.5%.[11]

- **"Front-end sales load"** occur when the fees and commissions to the selling broker are paid at the time the investor purchases the shares. This reduces the amount invested.

- **"Back-end sales load"** occur when the fees and commissions to the selling broker are paid at the time the shares are redeemed. In this way, all of the investor's money is at work. The fee is dependent upon the time the shares are held, the price paid, and the price at which they are redeemed.

- *Redemption:* These are not commissions but are paid to the fund to offset the costs of redemption when the shareholder redeems their shares. It is not considered a "load" and is limited to 2%.

- *Exchange:* Some funds charge shareholders a fee to exchange or transfer to another fund.

- *Account:* You might be charged a maintenance fee when the value of the account is below a certain value.

- *Purchase:* Paid to the fund to defray operating costs.

---

[10] Source: Moneylife, "Why people lose money in mutual funds," December 12, 2012
[11] Source: U.S. Securities and Exchange Commission, Mutual Fund Fees and Expenses

II. Annual fund operating fees

- *Management:* These are paid to the fund's investment advisor from the fund's assets for managing the fund's portfolio. They include administrative fees not included in "Other Expenses."

- *Service or 12b-1:* Paid from fund assets when the plan is adopted. Included expenses are marketing, selling, advertising, mailing, and printing of sales literature.

- *Other expenses:* Include legal, custodial, accounting, and other administrative expenses.

- For a number of reasons, including federal fee disclosure mandates, mutual fund fees have been trending lower since 1990 and 401(k) investors tend to buy lower-cost funds.

- In 2012, the average expense ratio on equity funds offered for sale in the United States was 1.40 %. 401(k) plan participants who invested in equity mutual funds paid less than half that amount, 0.63%. Bond fund expenses averaged 0.61%.[12]

It's vital that you understand the amount of commissions and fees you're paying on your investments. Most people fail to take costs into account when calculating their rate of return and are under the impression they are doing better than they really are.

III. Example of investment results with different fees:[13]

$10,000 invested at 10% for 20 years with a 1.5% operating expense = $49,725

Same amount invested with a 0.5% operating expense = $60,858

b) Average rate of return versus actual rate of return.

Many times you will see a particular stock or fund that has an "average rate of return" of X%. The average rate of return is calculated by dividing the overall rate of return by the number of years.

For Example:

You invest $1,000. Your rate of return is:

Year One = 100%:	Balance at the end of Year One is	$2,000
Year Two = 100%:	Balance at the end of Year Two is	$4,000
Year Three = Minus 50%:	Balance at the end of year Three is:	$2,000
Year Four = Minus 50%;	Balance at the end of year Four is:	$1,000

You finish up with the same amount of dollars that you started with: $1,000.

---

[12]   Source: Investment Company Institute, Research Perspective, Vol.19, No. 3, April 2013.
[13]   Source: U.S Securities and Exchange Commission, Mutual Fund Fees and Expenses.

> **Your Actual Rate of Return is 0.0%**
> **BUT**
> **Your Average Rate of Return** = 100%+100% − 50%–50% = 100% /4 years = **25%**

You will also hear about mean which is the same as average. Also Median is the middle number of a series of numbers; it means there are an equal number above the mean and an equal number below. It has nothing to do with averages.

c) Money markets

Money market funds invest in high quality, short-term securities. Their goal is to maintain a stable value while providing income.

- These are liquid assets designed for conservative investors.
- Currently, they are federally insured up to $250,000 per account.
- They generally offer a better interest rate than a conventional savings account.

d) Index funds

These investment funds seek to match the returns of a benchmark index and purchase all, or a representative sample, of the same securities as the benchmark index. Good examples of a benchmark index include, S&P 500, Dow Jones Industrial Average, Wilshire 500, and The Russell 2000.

- Passively managed to keep expense fees low.

e) Exchange-traded funds (ETF)

Exchange-traded funds are a portfolio of stock, bonds, and other investment instruments which trade as one stock, and are designed to match the return of an index, for example the S&P 500.

ETFs fluctuate throughout the trading day, meaning an investor could take advantage of a low price in the morning, and sell at a high price later in the day.

- Exchange-traded funds are passively managed so they have lower expense fees.
- Being market driven these funds can be volatile.

f) Open-end funds

These mutual funds have an unrestricted limit on the number of shares they can issue. The number issued usually depends on the demand. The funds also buy back shares when the investor wishes to sell, and this provides a ready investment conduit.

g) Closed-end funds

These are investment companies traded on the stock market that offer a fixed number of shares for sale at an initial public offering. Typically, the shares are then bought and sold on secondary markets such as NYSE or NASDQ from other individual investors.

- These are professionally managed funds.

- They are not required to maintain cash reserves, offering high flexibility in type of investment.

- Closed-end funds are not generally redeemable.

h) Unit investment trusts

These are investment companies that offer a fixed group of securities in the same way as a closed-end fund. But, the securities are held for a fixed period of time, and in this way investors can see what they are investing in over the period of time of the trust.

i) Hedge funds

These funds are often set up for the experienced investor as limited partnerships where the minimum investment can be $250,000 or more. Generally, they seek to manage risk by setting aside reserves to balance (hedge) against loss. This is not always the case, and there are numerous types of funds investing in numerous financial vehicles, often without the hedge. The investor generally pays a fixed management fee, and a percentage of the profit.

10. Retirement plans

a) Qualified and non-qualified plans

Qualified plans are set up by employers to provide retirement savings to their employees. They are overseen by ERISA (Employee Retirement Income Security Act) and the IRS. Rules and regulations are in place involving all aspects of the plan.

Non-qualified Plans are more loosely overseen by ERISA and the IRS, but offer much less in the way of tax advantages to both the employer and employee. They would include, deferred compensation plans, executive bonus plans, and split dollar insurance, among others.

The financial institutions have succeeded in creating a program where they automatically get your retirement money under their control for long periods of time, earning substantial fees and the use of your money, while giving you the impression that it's a great program. When you consider all of the disadvantages you may want to reconsider if it's a good strategy for you.

b) Common qualified retirement plan vehicles:

- **401(k)**: Used by most employers as a way of encouraging employees to save.

- **IRA**: There are approximately 11 different types of IRA plans. Each has different terms and conditions which can vary annually.

- **Roth IRA**: Whereas the 401(k) and the IRA plans involve tax-deductible contributions and tax deferral until distribution, Roth IRAs have no tax deduction but grow tax free and are not taxed at distribution.

- **403(b)**: (tax-sheltered annuity) is for the education and nonprofit sectors, but is similar to the 401(k).

- **The Roth 401(k)** has recently been introduced, but is not as frequently offered by employers as a traditional 401(k).

It should be noted that the recent bankruptcy filing in Detroit has had a chilling effect on public retirement programs. Unfunded pension programs are common, and it's a fact that many programs promise much more than they can ever deliver. It is likely that restructuring these plans will take place on a large scale to the detriment of participants, but no worse than the losses suffered in the private sector.

c) Traditional (qualified) plans: 401(k), 403(b) (TSA), and IRA

These are tax deferral vehicles. Your contributions are tax deductible. Taxes take place during later years, when you take your money out of the plan, generally at retirement.

The 403(b) is similar to a 401(k), but is used by public education and nonprofit groups. They typically invest in mutual funds or tax-sheltered annuities.

Although your qualified plan can be a defined benefit plan, most are defined contribution plans.

d) Advantages of a qualified plan:

- Employer match
- The contribution is tax deductible
- The fund grows on a tax-deferred basis
- Choice of investment funds
- This is a forced, systematic savings plan providing security at retirement.
- Everybody's doing it so it must be good.

e) Disadvantages of a qualified plan:

- You lose control of your money.
- You are penalized and taxed on withdrawals before 59.5 years of age, unless you qualify for one of a small number of exceptions.
- You are forced to take distributions at 70 ½ so there's no avoiding the taxes.
- Distributions are included as salary for social security, Medicare, and federal unemployment tax purposes.
- One principle behind these plans, is that you are in a higher tax bracket when you're younger than during your retirement years. Often, this is not the case because you build assets as you go through life and your tax bracket during retirement may actually increase.
- The government, as we have seen recently, may also increase taxes.
- Most 401(k) and IRA holders look at the total amount accumulated and don't anticipate the taxes on withdrawals.
- The highest income brackets in 2014 will see 39.6% going to the Feds, plus 0.9% for Medicare taxes, plus 3.8% on investment income. Added to this will also be another percentage going to the state.

- No preferential capital gain, its all ordinary income.

- State taxes apply to the state you are resident at the time of withdrawal. This has created a big attraction for retirees to consider states who have no state income tax. These include: Alaska, Florida, Nevada, South Dakota, Texas, and Washington.

- Costs and fees lower your rate of return substantially.

- Poor liquidity.

- There's no protection from death or disability.

- There is a limit on the amount you can contribute.

- It cannot be taken with you to other employment.

- The prospectus is very complex and not easily understood especially when it comes to fees.

You're probably surprised at the number of disadvantages as compared to the much trumpeted advantages from the financial institutions.

f) SEP IRA

This type of IRA allows an employer, typically a business owner or self-employed individual, to make contributions to an IRA in an employee's name.

g) SIMPLE IRA

For employers that have no other retirement plan. This type of IRA allows both employer and employee to make contributions. There are lower fees and lower contributions than a 401(k).

h) Roth IRA

You've already paid taxes on your contribution so there is no tax deduction. You contribute from your take-home pay. Your Roth fund is not tax deferred. It's tax exempt.

- There is no tax on any distribution, including any gain in value, providing the account is five years old or you are at least 59 ½ years old.

- There are no mandatory distributions rules.

i) Roth 401(k)

The introduction of the Roth 401(k) plan for employees where money grows on a tax-free basis seems preferable to the traditional 401(k). There are restrictions on the contributions, and it is less commonly offered than the traditional 401(k).

- The best strategy is to contribute enough to maximize your employer match.

- Providing you qualify by way of income, consider investing the balance of your investment contributions in a Roth IRA for flexibility of distribution, and larger choice of investment funds.

- The biggest advantage is the tax-exempt status during growth, and at distribution.

j) Employer matching funds

This is by far the biggest reason that people like retirement plans because they are regarded as free money. You will pay taxes on the employer match, whether it's in either a traditional or a Roth retirement plan.

- Make enough of a contribution to qualify for the employer's match in your retirement fund.

- Do not fund beyond your employer match until you have your safety net fully in place and have carefully considered the option of a taxable account.

k) Vesting

Vesting defines the time, and method used, to transfer the ownership of matching funds to you. Any contribution *you* make to your 401(k) plan is automatically vested.

Employers usually regard vesting as a way to reward valued employees and will usually use either:

- A cliff or a graded vesting schedule.

- The cliff schedule gives you 100% ownership after a period of time. For example three years of employment and participation in the plan.

- The graded schedule will award an annual percentage.

- You are fully vested after six years under either program.

One disadvantage of the cliff schedule is the potential loss of employer match when leaving a job. If you are only 50% vested in your plan, you have to consider your loss over the time before you become fully vested. It could be thousands of dollars.

l) Qualified plan savings when leaving your job

You can make a rollover contribution, (a tax-free distribution) from one retirement plan to another.

- It's a good strategy to have the plan administrators deal with the rollover because you do not want to receive the cash personally and face a possible tax liability as a result.

m) Employee stock options

These provide the holder with an option to purchase a number of shares for a pre-determined price at a pre-determined time. Usually the price of the share at the time the options are granted is the market price. The hope is that the price of the shares will increase in the future. At this time, the holder of the option can exercise the option, and purchase the shares. They can then be sold at the higher price, or held according to the investor's requirements.

- You have to be very careful of tax consequences regarding stock options.

11. Real estate investments

Real Estate investments are purchased for income, appreciation, and tax benefits. Prices and values differ widely according to location and should be considered on a local basis. This is a cursory look at a huge subject, worthy of a book on it's own.

- When purchased within budget, and planned for long-term investment, real estate is a very powerful asset.

- Since the end of World War II until the 1970s, purchasing a house was celebrated as buying a home. Today, for most homebuyers, it's also an investment with an expected rate of return.

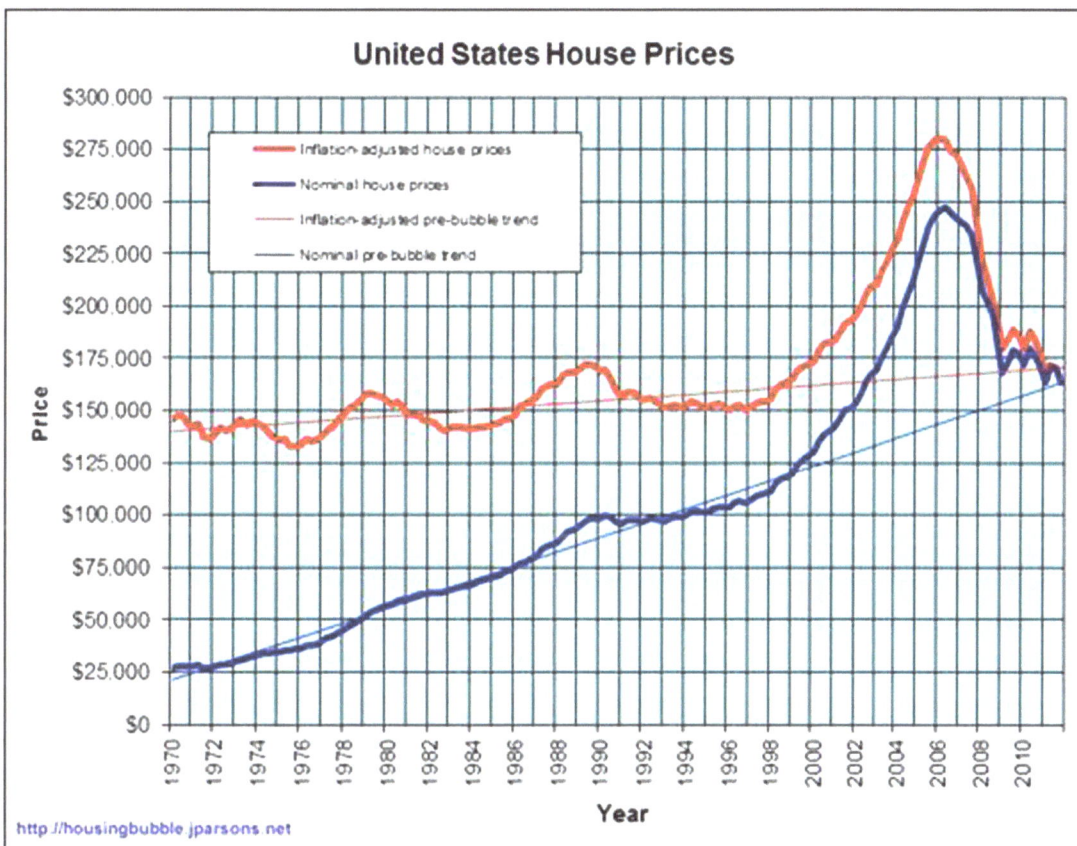

http://www.jparsons.net/housingbubble/

a) **Types of real estate investments:**

- Single family residences and up to four apartment units
- Apartment buildings with 5+ units
- Office buildings
- Industrial buildings
- Retail shopping centers and malls
- Research and development buildings
- Mobile home parks
- Land

b) **The advantages of owning real estate investments:**

- The interest paid on your mortgage is deductible for tax purposes.
- Appreciation. Over time, 20 years plus (sometimes much shorter), real estate will likely show an increase in value. Timing of, and planning for, appreciation is difficult with no guarantee of an increase in value, especially over the short term.
- The real estate market enjoys periods of time when the demand exceeds the supply and prices skyrocket.
- Cash flow: Many income properties provide a steady source of income for their owners.
- Income property provides a ready source of tax free cash from refinancing.
- Depreciation: Investors are allowed to deduct the building value of their investment properties over the course of years, for example, 27.5 years for residential income property. This is a true tax shelter.
- Compared to buying a house for rent to a tenant, buying more units, for example, five or more apartments, provides an economy of scale. A single house rental increase is one increase, whereas a five unit apartment rental increase provides five rent increases.

c) **Disadvantages of owning real estate**

Lack of liquidity. As we have witnessed since 2006, most real estate cannot be sold or refinanced without a loss especially in Florida, Nevada, and California. Similar booms and busts occur nationally about once per decade.

- Capital outlay: Investors typically need large sums of money to purchase income property and the operating expenses can be costly.
- Lack of financing: When banks are unwilling or unable to make loan there is a negative effect on property values.

- Management: With investment property, managing tenants, and negotiating rent and leases are not easy tasks, especially when the property is smaller and situated in another state.

d) **Return on investment for real estate**

Real estate investors look for a return in four different areas:

- Appreciation
- Depreciation
- Equity build up (loan principle pay down)
- Cash flow

The rate of return is calculated by adding the above four factors, and then dividing by the amount invested.

e) **Pricing real estate**

All real estate prices are subjective, housing particularly, because it is generally an emotional purchase governed by the ability of the purchaser to obtain a loan within their means. The following methods are in general use:

- **Comparable sales:** Finding similar properties that have sold in the same area. This is subject to the judgment of the person making the value assessment, especially on a single-family residence.

- **Gross income multiplier:** This is a very rough rule of thumb value. Multiplying the gross income by a factor, for example five times, will give a value. Obviously, the higher the factor, the higher the price.

- **Capitalization rate:** For commercial properties, values are also based on the percentage obtained from dividing the net operating income by the sales price. The net operating income is the gross income minus all expenses of running and maintaining the property including   a vacancy allowance but without including the mortgage expense. This provides a more accurate comparison of performance from like properties. A high capitalization (cap), rate means a higher price with a lower cash flow and a lower rate of return.

- **Price per square foot**

  You divide the purchase price by the total square footage. It's really part of a comparable sale analysis.

- For commercial property investors, cash-flow is king.

12. Collectibles

Investors generally buy collectibles for appreciation in value as well as appreciation of the art form. Timing the sale to maximize profit is difficult and depends on economic conditions.

Ferrari 275 GTB/4S NART Spyder

$15,000 new in 1967, $27.5 million in 2013[14]

The value of a collectible is usually affected by the general economy prevailing at the time of sale. Collectibles include:

- Artwork
- Cars
- Rugs
- Antiques
- Metals
- Gems
- Stamps
- Coins
- Fine wines and certain other tangible personal property.

---

[14] **Source:** Scott Reyburn - Aug 19, 2013, *Ferrari NART Spyder Sets $27.5 Million Auction Record, Bloomberg*

13. Chapter Two: Highlights

- Most people make the mistake of starting their financial life with investments. You increase your risk of financial loss exponentially when you grow wealth without a safety net.

- A safety net exists after you've taken care of basic financial risk to yourself, and your family, by putting safeguards in place should an unforeseen event occur. For example, emergency fund, protection against liability lawsuits, death, disability, hospitalization, out of date wills, and trusts.

- Investments, rather than savings, are a hedge against inflation where you take on more risk for more reward.

- The financial and political worlds are rife with corruption, collusion, and insider trading. This has a negative effect on your wealth by steering money that could be returned to you as profit into someone else's pocket.

- Asset diversification and asset allocation are strategies to balance your risk.

- There is a strong relationship between your emotions and investing, with markets being driven by fear and greed. Media hype supports these emotional highs and lows.

- Bonds are loans and are purchased for generating income that is sometimes tax-free.

- Stocks and shares are purchased to grow wealth and/or generate income. They are divided into common and preferred stock, with preferred stock receiving priority over common stock.

- Investing in a mutual fund is a way of pooling your money with a group of other investors to purchase stocks, bonds, and cash. There are literally thousands of funds.

- Mutual funds are classified as being either actively or passively managed. Actively managed funds try to *beat* the performance of a benchmark index. Passively managed funds try to *match* the performance of a benchmark index.

- From June 1998 through June 2013, only 25.6% of actively managed funds managed to beat their benchmark index, despite the fees and expenses being substantially higher than passively managed funds.

- Investment funds, which charge a fee, or commission, for each transaction, are called, load funds. Fees are deducted at the time of the investment.

- Some investment funds don't charge fees or commissions on transactions, and are called no-load funds. With a no-load fund the investor has the advantage that all of his money goes into the investment.

- Generally, investors know too little about the fees they pay for their investments. All fees lower your rate of return.

- Money market funds invest in high quality short-term securities which are liquid, federally insured up to $250,000, and generally offer a better rate of return than a savings account.

- Index funds are passively managed, and seek to match the returns of benchmark index, and purchase all or a representative sample of the same securities as in the benchmark index.

- Exchange-traded funds are a portfolio of stock, bonds, and other investments which trade as one stock, and are designed to match the return of an index, for example the S&P 500. They are passively managed funds to keep expenses low.

- Open-end funds issue an unrestricted number of shares while closed-end funds issue a limited number of shares.

- Unit investment trusts are similar to closed-end funds, but usually offer a fixed group of securities over a fixed period of time.

- Hedge funds are usually set up as limited partnerships and generally have a high level of investment. Investors typically pay a management fee and a share of the profits as fees.

- Most qualified retirement plans accumulate taxes as well as interest, for example IRAs and 401(k)s. Very often the tax bracket at distribution is higher than the tax bracket during contribution. This means that you are paying more in taxes. Roth IRAs and Roth 401(k)s are not subject to this major hole in the tax-deferred strategy.

- The disadvantages of a qualified retirement plan should be carefully considered along with the advantages.

- You should carefully consider whether you should contribute to a qualified retirement plan when you don't have an emergency fund. You are locking your money up, sometimes for 30 years, without being able to access it unless you pay a severe penalty.

- Employer matching funds are generally regarded as free money but you will pay taxes on that money at distribution whether it is a traditional qualified or a Roth plan.

- Consider limiting your contribution to a qualified retirement plan to obtain the employer match until you have your safety net firmly in place.

- Vesting describes the transfer of the ownership of employer matching funds to you. There are two common methods and you are automatically vested within six years under either method.

- On leaving your job you can roll your retirement plan into another but it's wise to avoid the possibility of tax consequences by using plan administrators to handle the transfer.

- Stock options can carry large tax consequences.

- Real estate is a powerful asset when purchased within budget for long-term investment. Income property is an outstanding investment when purchased under the same terms and conditions.

- Real estate is a tax-preferred industry with the interest on mortgages being tax deductible, as well as the tax advantages of depreciation and favorable treatment on capital gains tax.

- Since the 1970s, homeowners have regarded their houses as an investment with an expected rate of return as well as being their home.

- Advantages of owning real estate for investment include, tax advantages, appreciation, equity build up, and cash flow from rents.

- The main disadvantages of owning real estate are market unpredictability and lack of liquidity.

- Pricing real estate is subjective, especially for a single-family residence where comparable sales dominate the decision on price.

- Income property investors use comparable sales, gross income multipliers, and capitalization rates to price property. Cash flow is king.

- Collectibles are purchased for two forms of appreciation, value and the art form. Coins, autos, stamps, artwork, and other items are subject to the same market unpredictability as real estate.

chapter three:
m is for mortgages

SPEND A MAXIMUM OF 25% OF GROSS INCOME ON MORTGAGE PAYMENTS.

Chapter Three focuses on mortgages. Descriptions are provided for informational purposes only. Everyone's financial situation is different, and financial purchases should be tailored to the individual. There are no recommendations to purchase products from any particular company. You are strongly advised to consult with experts and licensed professionals, as well as to seek legal and accounting advice, before making your financial decisions.

1. Your mortgage budget

There seems to be much disagreement among financial experts about the amount of income you should spend on your mortgage. Some experts speak of a percentage of take-home pay, others about gross income. These estimations vary widely and can leave consumers confused.

All advisors caution against spending too much on a mortgage payment because, as the recent foreclosure epidemic has shown us, having an unaffordable mortgage causes financial disaster and misery.

Having 25% of your gross income dedicated to your mortgage payments would appear to be a conservative amount, allowing you to qualify for maximum mortgage affordability.

Commercial real estate investors tend to buy property based on its financial rate of return. Home buyers tend to buy based on emotional factors, for example: perfect kitchen, great neighborhood, close to great schools, wonderful yard, perfectly sized rooms, love the dining room, wood floors, new carpet, and other factors. These emotional decisions tend to make us want to buy something we may not be able to afford.

Buying a home is not just about the mortgage payment; there are the other costs as well:

- Taxes
- Insurance
- Homeowner fees
- Utilities

Maintenance and Repairs include:

- Landscaping
- Pool
- Plumbing
- Electrical
- Roof
- Decks
- Driveway
- Pest control
- Paint: interior and exterior

Plumbing and electrical repairs are particularly expensive as you probably are unable to do the work yourself. Replacing a roof will dig a big hole in your pocket. Pools are very expensive to maintain, and cost hundreds of dollars monthly for cleaning and supplies.

Unexpected costs can be frightening when most of your money is going toward your mortgage payment.

2. How much mortgage does the lender say I can have?

All lenders examine your ability to pay back your mortgage using the following two ratios. A ratio is the percentage of your income to your debt.

Lenders have the discretion to accept higher debt ratios dependent upon the borrower's ability to pay the loan. A larger down payment would be one reason a lender might accept a higher debt to income ratio.

a) Front-end ratio:

The Federal Housing Administration (FHA) allows no more than 31% of your gross income to be used for:

- Loan principle and interest
- Real estate taxes
- Homeowner's insurance

(Lenders other than the FHA are more conservative and use 28% as the front-end ratio.)

b) Back-end ratio:

The FHA allows no more than 43% of your income, including the mortgage payment, to be used for all other installment loans, including:

- Car loans

- Credit cards

- Child support

- Student loans

- Personal loans and most other installment loans. There are some exceptions on bills that will be paid off in 10 months or less.

- Bills **NOT** included in the back-end ratio include: income taxes, healthcare costs, home utility bills, insurance, phone, cable, and food.

- Don't confuse the front-end and back-end ratios with your FICO® credit score which is covered later in this chapter.

(Lenders other than the FHA are more conservative and use 41% as the back-end ratio.)

c) FHA example:

Front-end ratio:

> Borrowers gross monthly income....................$5,000

> Multiply gross monthly income by 31%..................$1,550

Using 4.5% interest rate on a 30-year mortgage you could obtain a mortgage amounting to $305,000.

FHA loans are insured and you will pay a mortgage insurance premium in addition to your mortgage payment.

Back-end ratio:

> Borrower's gross monthly income....................$5,000

> Multiply gross monthly payment by 43%.................$2,150

With this example, where the borrower's front-end ratio is maximized at $1,550 the borrower's other monthly debt payments cannot exceed $600.

3. If the FHA will allow me 31% as a mortgage expense why recommend 25%?

Do not maximize the amount of mortgage you can obtain, maximize your ability to pay your mortgage and live comfortably by obtaining one well within your buying power. Using 25% of your gross monthly income as a maximum mortgage payment is conservative.

Providing the lender agrees, the amount of mortgage you can afford to pay is a based on your individual situation. Being conservative is wise because you do not want to spend all of your income on your house. You are responsible for all of the costs related to your home, and it's always much more expensive than you anticipate.

4. Purchasing real estate

Typically, a real estate purchase consists of a number of different items:

- Price: This is the amount the buyer agrees to pay the seller for the real estate. On a home, the price is usually obtained by using comparable sales of similar properties in the same area. (See Chapter Two: Investing: Real Estate)

- Down payment: Usually in cash and a percentage of the sales price, anywhere between 3.5% and 25%, depending on the cash reserves of the buyer, and the demand of the lender.

- Mortgage: This is the difference between the price paid and the down payment. It consists of a loan from a financial institution, a private party and/or perhaps even the seller.

- Terms are variable and usually more flexible when a private party owns the mortgage.

- The media hype around rising or falling prices has a significant effect on the emotions of those looking to buy or sell. In a market when prices are increasing, buyers feel as though they will be missing out on a good thing unless they buy today. Similarly, sellers feel the emotional pressure when prices are falling.

- An increasing demand for real estate causes interest rates to rise.[15]

US home values over time
Index of sale prices of standard existing homes, adjusted for inflation; Index 1890 = 100

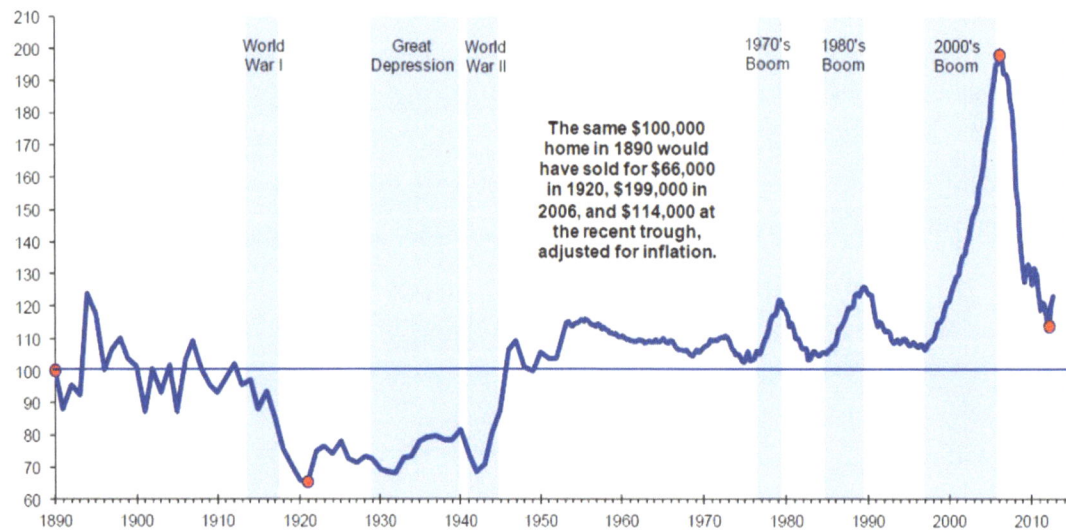

The same $100,000 home in 1890 would have sold for $66,000 in 1920, $199,000 in 2006, and $114,000 at the recent trough, adjusted for inflation.

Source: Robert J. Shiller, *Irrational Exuberance*, 2nd. Edition.

---

[15] Source: Graph: Robert J. Shiller, *Irrational Exuberance*, 2nd. Edition www.broadwaybooks.com

5. Tax savings

Loans secured by real estate have significant tax advantages. As a borrower, you are permitted to deduct the interest you pay on your loan from your gross income. This effectively lowers the amount of tax you pay. Your tax savings are the total amount of interest paid, multiplied by your tax bracket.

The tax savings on real estate loans makes real estate ownership a very attractive proposition. You are limited to deducting interest on more than $1 million used to construct, acquire, or improve a first or second home. You are also limited to interest deductions on $100,000 of loans on home equity and secondary loans.

6. Interest rates

The amount you borrow is only one part of the equation. The interest rate that you pay on the loan is just as critical because it influences the loan payment.

- Interest rates have steadily dropped over the last 30 years for all mortgage rates.
- The current economy has meandered since 2010 causing interest rates to rise and fall unpredictably. As interest rates increase, people seeking a loan will drop off. As interest rates fall, more people apply and are approved for their loans.[16]

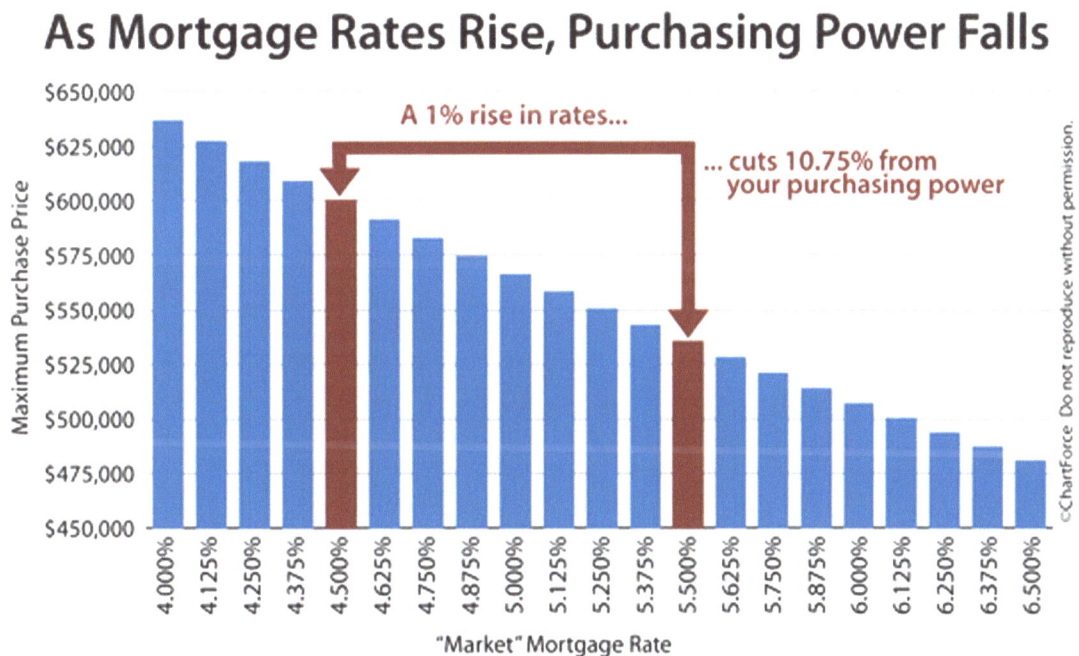

As Mortgage Rates Rise, Purchasing Power Falls

A 1% rise in rates... cuts 10.75% from your purchasing power

©ChartForce Do not reproduce without permission.

---

[16] Source: Dan Green, Waterstone Mortgage, Daily, The Mortgage Reports, June 2013

7. What is an APR (annual percentage rate) interest rate?

When you take out a loan it is paid off (amortized) using an interest rate and a period of time (term). There are often two interest rates quoted on a loan. One is the loan interest and the other, known as the annual percentage rate (APR), incorporates all the loan fees and costs. The APR should allow you to compare different mortgages, and their costs, on a level playing field. This is not necessarily so when you consider:

- The definition of APR can differ by state.
- Lenders do not have to include all fees in their APR.
- When you know what fees are included in the APR, you can comparison shop with confidence, comparing apples with apples.
- Advertised quoted interest rates are generally reserved for customers with the best credit.

8. Fannie Mae and Freddie Mac

Both organizations operate under a government charter to guarantee and purchase mortgages, which they either hold for their own portfolio, or sell to investors as mortgage-backed securities. Broadly, their purpose is to provide liquidity, stability, and affordability to the mortgage market. There are reportedly plans by President Obama to reorganize both, although details remain unclear.

Fannie Mae and Freddie Mac set standards for the loans they will either keep or sell, these include:

- A maximum amount of loan - for 2014 it is $417,000 with exceptions for high cost areas, where the loan limit is $625,000.
- Income requirement
- Down payment
- Credit
- Type of property

a) Conforming loans:

Loans, which meet the standards, set by Fannie Mae or Freddie Mac.

b) Non-conforming loans:

Loans which do not meet the standards of Freddie Mac and Fannie Mae are considered non-conforming. They are still funded through financial institutions often with higher interest rates. Common reasons for being a non-conforming loan are, lack of sufficient credit, exceeding the conforming loan limits, or for purchase of a second or investment property.

c) Jumbo loans:

A jumbo loan is one where the amount borrowed exceeds the limit set by Freddie Mac and Fannie Mae. Generally, interest rates are higher for these loans although the spread has narrowed in recent years.

9. The Federal Housing Administration (FHA)

The FHA is an insurance company for lenders, and provides protection against the risk of loss from defaults on mortgages secured by homes and other real estate. They have strict guidelines on the loans they underwrite:

- The FHA does not make loans. They set the standards by which they will insure a loan. The institutional lenders are actually making the loan.

- The cost of the mortgage insurance is usually added to the monthly loan payment.

- From June 2013, the mortgage insurance will be in place for no less than 11 years, and often for the life of the loan, dependent upon the amount of the loan to value of the property

FHA loan standards include:
- As low as 3.5% down payment (a much lower down payment compared to that of a conforming loan).

- A ceiling on the amount they will insure. Search for the county where you live, or wish to live. Loan limits vary widely according the property location.

- In 2013 the highest loan limit for a house was $729,750 which was in California including Los Angeles, Marin, Santa Clara, and Ventura Counties.

- Qualifying on these terms does not mean automatic acceptance. Credit history, stability of employment, and other factors are also taken into account.

10. Veterans Administration (VA) loans

The Veterans Administration governs loans under a program which guarantees loans, usually without a down payment.

- Military service requirement.

- No down payment

- The maximum loan amount differs by state and county.

- The maximum amount of loan in 2014 is $417,000 although there are some exceptions.

- No requirement for mortgage insurance.

11. Common types of home loans

Loans secured by real estate have changed dramatically over the past 40 years, with financial institutions introducing many different types of mortgages. One of the biggest changes included adjustable-rate mortgages, effectively lowering the interest rate and payment on a loan. This has enabled more people to purchase and spurred activity in the real estate market and, at the same time, the risk shifted from the financial institutions to the consumer.

These are the five most common mortgages you are likely to encounter:

- Fixed-rate mortgage
- Adjustable-rate mortgage (ARM) 1 year, 3 year, 5 year, or other
- Reverse mortgage
- Home equity
- Interest only

12. Fixed-rate mortgages

The interest rate and payment on the loan is fixed until the loan is paid off. The length (term) of the loan can vary between 10 and 50 years, although loans amortized (paid off) over 30 and 15 years are still the most popular.

a) Advantages include:

- Fixed monthly payments make it easy to fit into a budget.
- The interest rate and payment never change even in a volatile market where interest rates are quickly increasing. This provides stability to the borrower.
- Much easier to understand than an adjustable-rate mortgage.
- Allows the flexibility to make extra payments on the mortgage to shorten the amortization period, if the borrower elects to follow this strategy.

b) Disadvantages include:

- Fixed-rate mortgages have a higher interest rate than an adjustable-rate mortgage.
- Higher interest rates mean that it's harder for the borrower to qualify for the loan because the payments are higher.
- A higher interest rate can also mean you will be paying more for the home overall if your interest rate for a fixed-rate mortgage remains higher than an adjustable-rate mortgage.

c) **2012-2013 graph of interest rates on various mortgages**[17]

(Percent)

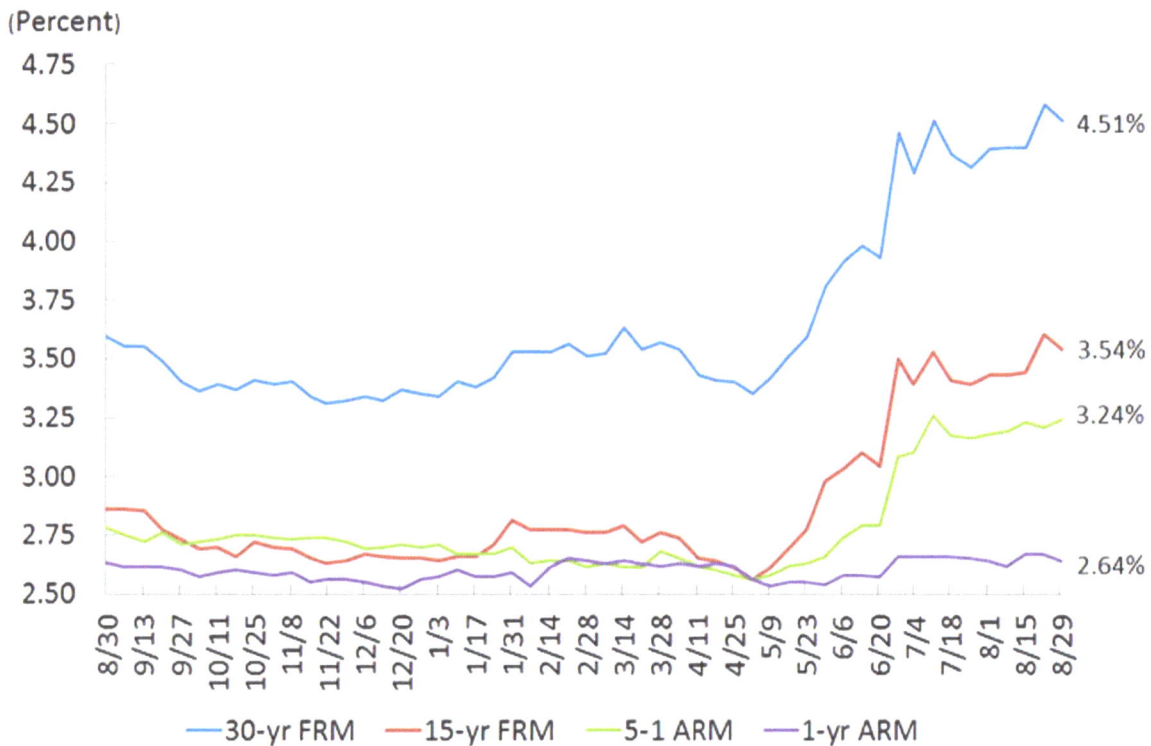

—30-yr FRM —15-yr FRM —5-1 ARM —1-yr ARM

Source: Freddie Mac

As of August 29, 2013

- The chart above shows the spread between a 30-year fixed-rate mortgage and a 15-year fixed-rate mortgage is lower than 1%.

- The spread between a 1-year ARM and a 30-year fixed-rate mortgage is almost 2%. For most borrowers, in a market where rates are increasing, this is probably not an acceptable risk just to obtain a larger mortgage.

- For the last few years, interest rates have been at historic lows. They show every sign of increasing in the future, especially when the economy recovers. You have to assess your situation and decide whether now is the time to take on the risk of an increase in interest rates from the lender to yourself with an ARM mortgage.

13. Fifteen-year mortgage versus thirty-year mortgage, what's best?

This strategy is the subject of much discussion and dispute among financial experts. And it can be a confusing picture for consumers.

- For most people there is no consideration, because the payments on the 15-year mortgage are far too high for their budget.

---

[17] Graph Source: Freddie Mac August 29, 2013

The decision on the right mortgage for you depends on your individual situation. It also depends on:

- The spread between the 30 and 15-year interest rate
- Your anticipated investment return
- Your tax bracket
- Your discipline to reinvest the dollars

For those who can afford the higher monthly payments the biggest advantages are:

- Paying off a loan over 15 years versus 30 years substantially reduces the amount of interest paid.
- The difference between the 15-year payment and the 30-year payment could be invested elsewhere after year 15. From 2004 – 2014, the before tax average S&P 500 return was approximately 7.3%
- You might be happier knowing that in 15 years your house is free and clear of mortgage debt, especially as you enter middle and late ages, freeing up the amount of the payment for investment or spending.
- There's some emotional satisfaction to freeing up the mortgage payment and be able to invest or spend it after 15 years.
- Most of any gain from investing in real estate will be treated as capital gain. Reinvesting the difference can be taxed at a higher level depending on your investment.

The biggest disadvantages include:

- With all the costs, tax savings, and investment considerations taken into consideration, paying a 15-year mortgage versus a 30-year mortgage is invariably more expensive over a 30-year time span. These considerations include:
- The 30-year payment offers substantially more tax savings on the interest paid. There is s a $1 million limitation on the loan for which interest can be deducted.
- With a 15-year mortgage, you quickly have a substantial amount invested in brick and mortar which is acknowledged as having liquidity weakness. This means that when you attempt to access the equity in your home, financial institutions may be unwilling or unable to make loans. Your income may be too low or too unstable, and you may have poor credit. Interest rates may also be too high to make it feasible.
- Inflation plays a part. A 30-year mortgage means that you are paying your mortgage with cheaper dollars than with a 15-year mortgage.
- You can get more real estate for your dollar with a 30-year loan because the payments are lower.

- With a 15-year mortgage you are locked into a high payment plan with no flexibility. The 30-year plan allows you the flexibility to make more than the required minimum payment if this strategy appeals to you.

- The investment lost opportunity costs on the additional payments for a 15 year mortgage are greater than the investment lost opportunity costs on the payments for years 15 through 30 on the 30 year mortgage.

14. Adjustable-rate mortgages (ARM)

These are mortgages where interest and payment rates vary throughout the term of the loan. The interest rates are usually linked to an index, and as the index changes up or down, so does the interest rate on your loan.

These loans are far more complicated than a fixed-rate loan because there are some many items that can affect your payment. A comparison sheet is attached below for your use when shopping for loans.

- An adjustable-rate mortgage effectively shifts the risk of an interest change from the lender to you.

- They are usually offered at a lower interest rate than a fixed rate. Lower interest rates are advantageous and you can buy more real estate for the same dollars.

- Typically ARM mortgages are amortized over 15 or 30 years.

- ARMs are quoted as 10/1, 5/1, 3/1, or whatever figure is appropriate. The first number is the time during which the interest and payment rate will be fixed. The second number is the frequency the interest rate will be adjusted after the fixed period. These are also known as hybrid loans because they incorporate both fixed and variable interest rates.

- For example: 3/1 ARM means that the rate is fixed for three years and the interest rate will adjust every year thereafter for the remaining term, 15 or 30 years.

a) **Typical ARM index types**

i. **LIBOR (London Interbank Offered Rate)**[18]

This is a frequently used index that tends to be more stable and has been a favorite among mortgage loan lending institutions. They are quoted on 3, 6, and 12 month rates. Generally a good index as it moves slowly in response to market changes.

In July 2013 the responsibility for this index was purchased from the British Bankers Association by NYSE Euronext, the company that operates the New York Stock Exchange.

---

[18] *As widely reported in the media, in an ongoing investigation, the Libor Index has been the subject of manipulation by a number of financial institutions for their profit*

Individually, we have no influence over either the index rate or corruption. This is a good reminder that being protected from the worst is your best defense.

ii. Treasury bills

ARMs are often tied to the 6-month Treasury bill rate. Treasury bills are regarded as a poor index because they can change rapidly, making it a fairly volatile index.

iii. 11th District cost of funds (COFI)

This index is the weighted average of interest rates of checking and savings account within the 11th Home Loan Federal Bank District savings institutions. This area covers most of the southwestern states. A good index in that it moves slowly in response to market changes.[19]

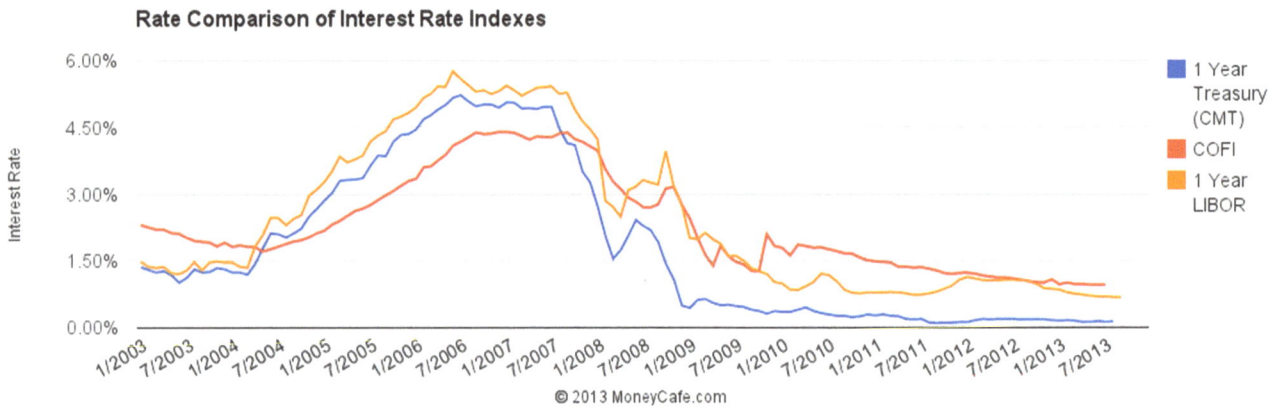

Rate Comparison of Interest Rate Indexes

© 2013 MoneyCafe.com

a) ARM interest margins

Interest rates on variable interest loans are linked to an index. Lenders use any number of indexes on which they base your rate. As the index goes up, so does your interest rate, and as the index goes down your rate may go down too.

Normally, you pay a percentage over the index rate as the interest rate on your loan called the **"*margin*."**

For example, the index rate may be at 0.75%. Your margin may be set at 2.75% above the index rate.

Index Rate	= 0.75%
+ Margin	= 2.75%
Interest Rate	= 3.5% (*Known as the "fully-indexed rate"*)

Index rate increased to 3.0%

+ Margin	= 2.75%
Fully-Indexed Rate	= 5.75%

It's worth noting that the margin can be lower for those with better credit.

---

[19] Source: Generous Media, Money Café 2013: Moneycafe.com

c) Interest rate caps:

There are usually limits on the amount an ARM interest rate and the payment rate can change; these are called a *"caps."*

    i. Periodic adjustment cap: Limits the amount the interest rate can be adjusted, up or down, from one adjustment period to another.

    ii. Lifetime cap: Limits the interest rate increase over the lifetime of the loan.

    iii. Carryover: With some interest rate caps, your rate and payment might be less than what it would have been if the index rate had been fully applied. The difference might be applied at the next adjustment period so your payment and rate might increase, even though the index decreases or remains the same.

d) Payment rate caps:

    i. Negative amortization: When the interest rates increases, the payment increase may be limited by a cap. As you are not required to increase the payment, any additional unpaid interest remaining is added to the principle amount.

    ii. Recast: Normally ARMs have a recalculation period, generally every five years, when the loan is recast to amortize the balance owed over the remaining loan term. This means your payment could increase substantially.

e) How do I know I can afford an ARM Mortgage over the long term?

When considering an ARM, it's a good idea to increase the interest rate and/or payment to its maximum limit over the minimum time limit, it caps. If, because of market conditions, this became a permanent change, ask yourself the following questions:

- Can I still comfortably afford the mortgage payment?

- Will I struggle to make the payment?

- What's the effect on the rest of my finances? On my savings? On my life's priorities; personal, professional, and financial?

f) Comparing Mortgages: Questions to have answered [6]

Mortgage Shopping Worksheet		
Name of lender		
Mortgage amount		
Mortgage type: fixed, 5/1 ARM, etc.		
Mortgage term: 15 years/30 years, etc		
Basic features for comparison		
Fixed-rate interest rate and APR		
ARM features		
ARM initial interest rate and APR		
How long does the initial rate apply?		
What will the interest rate be after the initial period?		
How often can the interest rate adjust?		
What is the index?		
What is the current rate on the index?		
What is the margin on this loan?		
What is the periodic interest rate cap?		
What is the lifetime interest rate cap?		
How low could the interest rate go on this loan?		
What is the payment cap?		
Can this loan have negative amortization?		
What is limit on the loan balance before recalculation?		
Is there a prepayment penalty?		
How long does the penalty last?		
How much is it?		
Is there a balloon payment on this loan?		
What is the estimated amount of the balloon payment?		
When would it be due?		
What is the total of all fees and points for this loan?		
What's my monthly payment the first year?		
What's my monthly payment after 1 year if the index stays same?		
Goes up 2%?		
Goes up 3%		
What is my maximum monthly payment after 1 year?		
What is my minimum monthly payment after 1 year?		
What is my maximum monthly payment after 3 years?		
What is my minimum monthly payment after 3 years?		
What is my maximum monthly payment after 5 years?		
What is my minimum monthly payment after 5 years?		
(6) Source: Board of Governors of the Federal Reserve System: Consumer Handbook on Adjustable Rate Mortgages		

15. Interest-only loans & balloon payments

These types of loans are most often found in commercial real estate lending, but some ARMS also have an interest-only provision with balloon payments.

- Interest (either fixed or variable) is paid on the outstanding loan balance until the term (5, 10, 15 years) expires.
- The whole balance of the loan becomes due and payable (a balloon payment) when the term expires.

- By avoiding paying principal on the loan, the borrower has lower loan payments for the term of the loan.

The payment of the balloon payment, at the end of the term of the loan, often comes down to timing. There can be obstacles including:

- Are banks willing to refinance?

- Are the banks able to refinance?

- Are economic conditions favorable or unfavorable for either?

16. Home equity loans

These fall into two types:

a) **Home equity loan:** a second mortgage on your home. This is usually funded with a lump sum of money, and at a fixed-interest rate.

b) **HELOC, a home equity line of credit.** More like a credit card where you access the money as you need it at a variable rate of interest. Usually a short-term loan that rolls over annually.

- Both are limited by a total loan to value ratio of between 75% and 85% of the value of your home including the first mortgage.

- Fees, closing costs, and interest rates can prove very expensive.

- If you cannot repay the loan, you risk losing your property.

- Think the process through carefully, understand the reasons you're taking the loan, and how you're going to afford to pay it back.

c) **Deductible interest:**

If all of your mortgages fit into one or more of the following three categories at all times during the year, you can deduct all of the interest on those mortgages. For more information in loan interest deductibility see IRS publication 936.

i. Mortgages you took out on or before October 13, 1987 (called grandfathered debt)

ii. Mortgages you took out after October 13, 1987 to buy, build, or improve your home (called home acquisition debt), but only if throughout 2012 these mortgages, plus any grandfathered debt totaled $1 million or less ($500,000 or less if married filing separately)

iii. Mortgages you took out after October 13, 1987 other than to buy, build, or improve your home (called home equity debt), but only if throughout 2012 these mortgages totaled $100,000 or less ($50,000 or less if married filing separately) and totaled no more than the fair market value of your home reduced by (1) and (2)

17. Refinancing

Most people refinance to get a more favorable loan by lowering their interest rate or to move from an ARM in a rising interest rate market to a fixed-rate mortgage. Consolidation of debt is another big reason behind a refinance.

- Determining your reason for a refinance is important because the payment savings will be offset by the costs of obtaining a new mortgage.

- According to Bankrate's 2013 closing cost survey, the national average for closing costs on a $200,000 loan was $2,402. The fees in the survey don't include taxes, insurance, or prepaid items such as prorated interest or homeowner association dues.[20]

- This means that a monthly payment savings of $200 would take about 18 months before you reach a breakeven point.

- Deduction of interest may be limited, see Paragraph 16 c) iii, above.

18. Prepayment Penalties

Lenders may want to charge a prepayment penalty when you pay off the loan before its due date.

- The penalty is usually triggered when the loan is paid off within three to five years after it was funded.

- The fee can be high. Six months of interest on the full loan amount is common.

19. Reverse mortgages

People aged 62 and over may have sufficient equity in their home to qualify for a loan but their lack of income may prevent them from obtaining one. With a reverse mortgage, the bank lends money to the borrower, secured by the equity in the property. The payment may be either a lump sum, monthly payments, or annual payments.

- The borrower makes no payment on the loan as long as they continue to live in the property. Taxes and insurance must be kept current.

- The loan balance is due when the owner dies, sells, or no longer resides in the property as their principal residence. At this time, the loan may be either refinanced or paid off from other assets. Otherwise, the house is sold to pay the debt. Any remaining balance would go to the next of kin.

- The FHA program has a home equity conversion mortgage (HECM) which insures that the lender will be compensated should the reverse mortgage payments exceed the value of the property when sold.

- Reverse mortgage loans are usually non-recourse loans, meaning that borrowers are not responsible should the property value be lower than the loan amount.

---

[20] Source: "When to refinance your mortgage" By Dr. Don Taylor, Ph.D., CFA, CFP, CASL • Bankrate.com www.bankrate.com/finance/mortgages/when-to-refinance-your-mortgage-1.aspx

- Payments to the borrower are loan advances and are not taxable.

- As of January 2014, qualifying for a reverse mortgage has become more difficult. This includes mortgage insurance increases, credit history consideration, and the ability to pay, also set asides for property taxes and hazard insurance have been put in place.

- There are significant costs including mortgage insurance premiums, points, and fees.

20. Reading and understanding your mortgage

Loan documents, insurance policies, and legal documents are boring to read and the use of industry related jargon doesn't help. Take the time to read the loan documents thoroughly and understand what they mean. Understand your options.

- You need to understand the contract wording because each lender defines their own terminology.

- Consult your professional advisor when you have questions. (See Chapter Four: Planning)

21. Your Credit: The real cost of bad credit

We all know that good credit offers us better loan terms than bad credit. (Also see Chapter One: Savings).

Here's a mortgage example:

    a) Man A (Good Credit)

$200,000 home loan amortized over 30 years at 4%

Monthly mortgage payment is $954.83

    b) Man B (Poor Credit)

$200,000 home loan amortized over 30 years at 6%

Monthly mortgage payment is $1,199.10

Man B pays $244.27 more a month for the same loan. Over 30 years that amounts to $87,937.20.

If Man A had invested that money monthly at 4% compounding over that period of time he would have made $169,535.45.

Poor credit can be the difference of being broke and having extra money in your pocket.

Solution

Man B should research his credit before he obtains his loan. He might be able to correct any credit flaws, improve his rating, reduce his interest rates, and save on his monthly payment.

22. FICO®

FICO® (Fair Isaac Corporation) is a standard used by credit agencies to measure your creditworthiness.

- Your score (on a scale up to 850 with 850 being best) is dependent upon a number of factors including payment and length of credit history.

- Scores can vary depending upon which credit agency is reporting, but good credit will always be rewarded with lower interest rates and better terms.

23. You have to pay to get your FICO® score

There are three main credit agencies in the US; Equifax, Experian, and TransUnion. Credit agencies may report a different score because of the way they assess your credit profile. All credit reporting agencies are required by law to supply you with a free credit report annually.

BUT

- You will have to pay a fee to each credit reporting agency to obtain their FICO® score for you. That's three fees to get a score from the three dominant agencies.

You can get an idea of your FICO® score at no cost.

- Free online sources allow you to enter broad details of your credit history. The information you enter does not identify you personally and allows you to obtain a low and high FICO® score range based on the information provided.

24. Improving your credit score

Order a copy of your credit report to see how your credit can be improved.

- One of the main criteria affecting your credit score, is the amount of debt you are carrying versus your income. Reducing your debt and/or increasing your income will improve your score.

- Consistently paying your bills on time can cause significant improvement in your credit score within a year.

- Paying a fee to get your FICO® score will allow you to review your credit in detail and indicate where your credit is deficient.

- If you can, pay down your debt so that credit available is far higher than any outstanding balance.

- Keep all old accounts open because a long credit history is important. Use them on a regular basis for small purchases.

- Unpaid bills sent for collection, and even one late payment, can have a huge negative impact on your credit. Pay your bills on time.

- Paying the minimum payment on a credit card also raises a red flag with the credit agencies. Pay at least few dollars over the minimum payment which reflects the interest charged. The additional dollars will help pay down the principal.

- Make sure your credit report is accurate and work with former creditors to remove any adverse comments that are outdated.

25. Waiting periods for bad credit

Applying for a mortgage with a poor credit history (derogatory events) usually involves the requirement of a waiting period before an application will be considered. This period depends upon some of the following criteria:

- The lender insuring the loan: FHA, VA, Fannie Mae, Freddie Mac

- Any extenuating circumstances

- The type of poor credit on the report, a short sale or foreclosure for example

- Your FICO score

- Loan to value ratio

- For example, with a Chapter 7 or 11 bankruptcy under a Fannie Mae insured loan, you may have to wait as long as four years, whereas with an FHA loan you may only have to wait two years

- Short sales, a deed in lieu of foreclosure, and foreclosure, all have waiting times from two to seven years.

- Extenuating circumstances such as job loss or illness can mitigate the waiting times.

- Foreclosure, short sales, and deed in lieu, are treated more sympathetically if the house had a mortgage substantially in excess of its value and there was financial hardship.

Lenders will also be looking for a positive credit history, stable income, low debt to income, and an adequate down payment.

26. Your liability if you don't make your mortgage payments

These are subjects to laws which vary from state to state and change frequently.

- Mortgage loans are secured by your real estate, normally your home. When you make the decision to stop paying your mortgage payments the lender looks to the sale of your home to collect the mortgage owed.

- Lenders usually allow 3 months of delinquency before taking action to foreclose on the property, although they will usually file a notice of default after the first payment is missed.

- States vary in their treatment of mortgage loans; some states classify loans as recourse loans where the borrower is personally liable for the loan. Other states classify loans as non-recourse loans where the borrower is not personally liable for the loan.

- Lenders can often no longer look to the value of the home to recover their losses especially where there are several loans on the property.

- Mortgages often exceed the value of the home and are referred to as being "underwater." The difference in the amount the lender receives, and the amount owed, is called a loan deficiency

- Should the borrower be a resident in a state where the mortgage is classified as a recourse loan, the borrower is personally liable for the deficiency, and the lender could sue and obtain a judgment against the borrower. Some lenders pursue this option aggressively, obtaining wage garnishment, bank levies, or other forms of recourse. Your only option may be bankruptcy.

- If you want to keep your home, there are mediation laws in effect requiring lenders to renegotiate your loan terms.

- Several years ago, the IRS could tax you on the amount of the mortgage deficiency but The Mortgage Forgiveness Debt Relief Act of 2007, which expired in December 2013 stopped this tax on mortgage relief with some limitations. The current position on an extension of the Act, offering continued protection, is unclear in June 2014.

a) Short sale:

This occurs when a buyer and seller agree to a sales price below the value of the existing mortgage. If the lender agrees to take the lower amount as full settlement a short sale takes place.

- Very often the short sale process allows the lender in first position to collect most, if not all, of their loan.

- Other lenders may not be as lucky and may be more aggressive about collecting the deficiency if allowed. You could end up having a judgment recorded against you, and be in a collection account, or forced into bankruptcy, all for a loan on a property you no longer own.

- Short sales conducted under HAFA (Home Affordable Foreclosure Alternatives Program) are excluded from a deficiency judgment.

- Get legal and expert advice. Know your options. You should obtain a written agreement from the lenders that they will not take further collection action after the short sale occurs.

b) Deed in lieu of foreclosure

This occurs when you voluntarily surrender the keys of the property to the lender and receive forgiveness of the loan. Most states do not have laws preventing your liability for the deficient amount of the mortgage if there is a deficiency.

- A deed in lieu of foreclosure conducted under HAFA (Home Affordability Foreclosure Alternatives Program) is excluded from a deficiency judgment.

Generally, both the short sale and the deed in lieu of foreclosure have a lesser impact on your credit than a foreclosure.

c) Foreclosure:

There are two type of foreclosure:

i) Judicial foreclosure

Judicial foreclosure requires a court hearing. If this is successful, a sale by auction in a public place happens with the property being sold to the highest bidder, often the lender.

ii) Non-judicial foreclosure

This does not require a court hearing. Notice of default is filed, and if the borrower does not bring the mortgage current, this is followed by a notice of sale. These are recorded with the county recorder, along with public notices posted. When the appropriate period of notice expires, a public auction is held, and the property is sold to the highest bidder.

In some states the foreclosure process prevents a lender from pursing the borrower for the loan deficiency.

- Late payments, short sales, and foreclosures remain on your credit report for as long as 7 to10 years.

- Effectively this means that you are either not able to get credit, or the credit offered has higher interest rates and fees. This will last all the while the report remains on your credit.

- In all these cases you should know who has the responsibility for the loan.

- Just because you are married and have community property does not mean you have equal liability. It is the person(s) who signed the loan documents who has the liability.

In all cases, you are advised to seek the advice of legal and accounting experts. Individual circumstances differ, but you need to know all of your options so you can make an informed decision.

27. Chapter Three: Highlights

- There is much disagreement among financial advisors and experts about the amount of money you should spend on your housing. Some speak of a percentage of net income and others a percentage of gross income. However, all caution against spending too much because this is long-term debt and an unaffordable mortgage causes financial disaster and misery.

- Twenty-five percent of gross income toward mortgage payments is recommended. It's not your ability to maximize your loan amount, but your ability to maximize your ability to repay the loan that's important.

- Buying a home is an expensive proposition, it's not just a mortgage payment. The other significant costs include; taxes, insurance, utilities, landscaping, electrical, plumbing, roof, decks, driveway, pest control, and interior and exterior paint. Many of these expenses are ongoing maintenance expense items.

- Homes are purchased based on emotional appeal. As such, buyers are pressured into buying something they really cannot afford because it meets their emotional needs.

- Lenders use two ratios of expense to income to determine the amount of mortgage you can afford.

- The front-end ratio determines the percentage of your gross income to be used for loan principle and interest, real estate taxes, and homeowners insurance. The Federal Housing Administration (FHA) uses 31% and other lenders use 28% of your gross income.

- The back-end ratio takes into account all debt including the mortgage payment. This would include credit card debt, student loans, child support payments, and most installment loans. The FHA allows 43% and other lenders use 41% of your gross income.

- Not included in the back-end ratio are income taxes, healthcare costs, and utility bills.

- The media hype surrounding increasing or decreasing home sales has a significant effect on the emotions of buyers and sellers.

- An increasing demand for real estate causes interest rates to increase.

- Loans secured by real estate enjoy significant tax advantages although there are some limitations on the deductibility on the interest on loans of $1 million and above, as well as home equity and secondary loans in excess of $100,000.

- The interest rate on mortgage loans has steadily dropped for the past 30 years but since 2010 have remained fairly constant with small increases followed by small decreases.

- The annual percentage rate (APR) is designed to show the interest rate with all costs. This should allow a fair comparison of loan interest rates but that may not be the case. Advertised rates are generally reserved for the best customers, the definition of APR can differ by state, and lenders do not have to include all fees in the APR.

- Fannie Mae and Freddie Mac operate under a government charter to guarantee and purchase mortgages which they either sell or hold for their own portfolio.

- Conforming loans generally meet the standards set by Fannie Mae and Freddie Mac, but non-conforming loans do not. Jumbo loans generally exceed the limits set by Freddie Mac and Fannie Mae and often incur a higher interest rate.

- The Federal Housing Administration (FHA) is an insurance company insuring lenders from default on mortgages. They do not make loans themselves.

- Since June 2013, the cost of insuring the loan is added to the mortgage payment and is in place for no less than 11 years, and can be for the life of the loan, dependent upon the loan to value.

- FHA loans can be obtained with as little as a 3.5% down payment, but the ceiling on the total loan amount depends on the county and state where the property is located. Credit history and employment stability are taken into consideration, so qualifying for a low down payment does not mean automatic acceptance.

- The Veteran Administration (VA) also guarantees loans, usually without a down payment. The maximum loan amount differs by state and county, and there is no requirement for mortgage insurance.

- Fixed-rate mortgages offer a fixed interest rate and payment for the duration of the loan which can vary between 10 and 40 years. However, 30-year and 15-year mortgages remain the most popular fixed-rate mortgage terms.

- Having a fixed rate and fixed monthly payment has the advantage of being a stable expense, easily accommodated by any budget especially in a volatile market. They are much less complex and more easily understood than a variable-rate mortgage.

- On the downside, the monthly payment is higher than for an adjustable-rate mortgage making qualification for the loan more difficult. The higher interest rate also means you will eventually pay more for your home than with using an adjustable-rate mortgage should the fixed rate remain significantly higher than the adjustable rate.

- When the economy recovers, the likelihood of an increase in interest rate is high. One decision to be taken into consideration is shifting the risk of an increasing interest rate (and monthly payment) away from the lender to you by taking on an adjustable-rate mortgage.

- There is much discussion about the 30-year versus the 15-year mortgage, and which is best. For the vast majority of people this is a non-starter because they cannot afford the payment increase caused by paying off and qualifying for a mortgage for 15 years as opposed to 30 years.

- For those who can afford it, the concept is one of obtaining a 15-year mortgage and paying much less for your home because you are paying much less interest than with a 30-year loan. This is only part of the picture. And careful consideration must be given to the interest rate spread, tax savings, investment returns, and inflation. Generally, mathematically, a 30-year mortgage is cheaper than a 15-year mortgage when considered over a 30-year time span.

- An adjustable-rate mortgage (ARM) is a mortgage where the interest and payment rate vary during the term of the loan. They are offered at a lower rate than a fixed-rate mortgage. Effectively, the risk of changes in the interest rate, especially an increase, is shifted from the lender to the borrower.

- The interest rate charged is linked to an index. Examples include, LIBOR, Treasury Bills, and 11th District cost of funds. The interest rate charged is usually a set amount, called a margin, above the indexed rate. As the index moves so does the interest rate.

- ARMs have interest and payment maximums called caps. These limit the timing and the rate of increase over the term of the loan. It is possible to owe more than you borrow when the interest rate rises quickly and you do not pay enough to amortize the loan over its term. This is called negative amortization.

- Affording an ARM over a period of time can be judged by increasing the interest and payment rates to their maximum over the minimum amount of time. You can now assess your comfort level with the higher payment and its effect on the rest of your financial picture.

- Interest-only loans are loans where the borrower literally pays only the interest on the loan. At the end of the loan term the borrower has to pay the remaining loan balance, commonly known as a balloon payment. The economic picture, and the bank's lending practices, can be a huge disadvantage at the time the balloon payment is due.

- Home equity loans are of two types. One is a secondary mortgage secured by your home, and the other, a home equity line of credit (HELOC) is a line of credit also secured by your home.

- Deduction of loan interest for tax purposes might be limited in the refinance process.

- When a loan is paid off prior to its due date, especially during the first 5 years of the loan, the lender may feel that their investment is harmed and impose a penalty. This is called a prepayment penalty, and often amounts to 6 months of interest on the loan.

- Homeowners aged 62 or more may qualify for a reverse mortgage, where the bank lends money to the borrower. It is secured by the real estate, but subject to certain conditions, and requires no payment from the homeowner. The money can be in the form of a lump sum or a series of monthly payments. The loan is repaid when the homeowner moves or dies, and either from other assets, or by sale of the home.

- Commencing in 2014, qualifying for a reverse mortgage became more difficult with credit history, property taxes, and hazard and mortgage insurance all becoming part of the consideration.

- FICO (Fair Isaac Corporation) has created a standard measurement used by lenders to establish credit worthiness. Although the three main credit reporting agencies are, by law, required to give you a free credit report annually, you have to pay to get a FICO score.

- One of the main factors affecting credit score is the amount of debt you carry versus your income. Reducing your debt and/or increasing your income will improve your score.

- Other factors improving your credit score include, paying your bills on time, with just one late payment having a huge adverse affect. Also, avoid paying just the minimum payment.

- Reviewing your credit score annually allows you to clear up adverse and misreported credit discrepancies.

- Failure to make mortgage payments according to the terms can result in one of four situations: a short sale, a deed in lieu of foreclosure, a judicial foreclosure, or a non-judicial foreclosure. In trust deed states like California, there is no court hearing. Normally, the property is sold to compensate the lender, but on many occasions the sale price is less than the loan amount. This difference is called a loan deficiency.

- For those with derogatory credit, a waiting period is applied before you can apply for a loan insured by the FHA, VA, Fannie Mae, or Freddie Mac. These periods can be anywhere from two to seven years and depend on the lender, the type of derogatory credit, your FICO score, extenuating circumstances, and loan to value.

- Borrowers must make themselves aware of all of their options to avoid being liable for the loan deficiency despite not owning the property. Consideration must also be given to being liable for potential income tax liability on the "forgiveness" of the loan amount.

- In all cases, you are advised to seek legal and accounting experts when obtaining a loan. The services of a qualified and licensed mortgage broker are also very important. Mortgage terms, conditions, and rates change daily. Explore all options so that the decisions you make are informed ones and the best for you.

chapter four
p is for planning

Chapter Four focuses on planning. Descriptions are provided for informational purposes only. Everyone's financial situation is different, and financial purchases should be tailored to the individual. There are no recommendations to purchase products from any particular company. You are strongly advised to consult with experts and licensed professionals, as well as to seek legal and accounting advice, before making your financial decisions.

1.   Why should I have a financial plan?

As we saw in Chapter One: Savings, the lifetime earnings calculation is very important because it gives us the approximate amount of dollars that will flow through our hands during our lifetime.

If you make $75,000 annually for 40 years (aged 25 – 65), your lifetime earnings are $3,000,000. Take away state and federal taxes of 25% and you are left with about $2,250,000 with which to live, raise a family, save for retirement, pay college education, vacation and other expenses.

- What is your lifetime earnings expectation? It's a good number to know.

Understanding that there is a limit to your lifetime income, that every dollar has to be conserved and planned for, is the first step to understanding, and controlling, your financial world.

*Visit www.simplifyourlife.com **and calculate your lifetime earnings.***

2.   Three challenges to achieving your financial priorities

a)   Time

The pressure of everyday life consumes time quickly. As you progress through life, time seems to go faster, compounding the sense that there's never enough time to get everything done. This is especially true when raising a family with all the commitments required by children for their extracurricular activities.

- Why do I work? You work to make money. Money allows you to support a lifestyle that will enable you to live, raise a family, and retire in some comfort. Many of you may have higher ambitions, but in either case, you are probably working many hours a week, taking little time off, travelling, and putting out the extra effort to keep your job.

- Do I have the wrong focus? Most people concentrate on earning money, but spend too little time examining and tracking their financial decisions. This is fatal flaw with a limited resource such as money.

b) Complexity

Think of your financial life as a big pond. Whenever you make a financial decision it's like throwing a pebble in the pond. The ripple affects the whole pond. To make sure it's not a tsunami of financial disaster, you need to fully understand how every financial decision affects your pond.

- Financial companies offer you thousands of different products, each claiming to solve your financial challenges. For example, 401(k) plans for retirement, 529 plans for college education, mutual funds for wealth accumulation, insurance for protection, mortgages for home purchase, and others.

- A multitude of financial product choices, with their respective claims on performance, makes choosing the right one for you much more complicated.

c) Action

You construct the 'great plan' and spend hours, days, weeks, and months on the design. Your plan, any plan, is only as good as the action taken to complete the plan. It's kind of like dieting, all enthusiasm at the beginning, with a drop off as self-discipline drops off.

- Consistency is the real key to success.

- This stuff is hard. Get help where you can.

No Time + Complexity + No Action = Muddled and confused decision making

3. When should I start to plan my finances?

Now! Gathering all of the relevant financial information is likely to be your first challenge. You will probably undergo a frustrating and time-consuming task of retrieving scattered records that are stuffed in piles with little organization to them. Sound familiar?

- Begin with the budget and cash-flow analysis discussed in Chapter One: Savings.

- People who have a good filing and records system have put themselves in the driver's seat. (See Chapter One, Savings)

- Year-end planning is good. New Year, new start.

- January 1 through the April 15 tax return time, provides a great opportunity for your annual review, being the most likely time you have your records together.

4. What's the best plan?

If you could create the best financial plan, here's how it would probably look:

- You would fund the plan with regular contributions.
- The money would earn a competitive return.
- The money contributed to the plan would grow tax free.
- The distribution would be tax free.
- There would be no penalty for accessing your money in the plan.
- There would be a provision guaranteeing no loss of capital.
- Risk would be minimized.
- The plan would be flexible and allow change when required.
- There would be protection from creditors.
- Provisions for death, sickness, emergencies, and any unforeseen factors would be included.
- You would control the plan, the government would not control it.

Buying products geared toward achievement of your financial priorities should meet most or all of these criteria.

Try matching your current financial products and strategies against this list, and you are likely to be disappointed with their performance.

5. The basic flaws in traditional financial planning

The needs approach

Many financial plans created today depend on a linear (straight line) approach based on the needs of the subject.

This approach is loosely based upon the answers to 3 questions:

1. How much money do you need to live on when you retire?
2. How much money are you willing to invest on a regular basis?
3. What amount of risk are you prepared to take?

The linear needs approach works backwards from the income you ***need*** in retirement to calculate your monthly contribution today, using interest rates and risk profiles.
The needs approach has some major flaws:

Linear needs planning places limits on your possibilities. Planning to maximize the best and most efficient use of your money is a better approach.

- You likely have an unrealistic and optimistic rate of return on your investments.

- Often, the assumption is that everything will work out as you've planned. When the market drops below your anticipated rate of return, it has to work twice as hard to catch up.

- You tend to increase risk, rather than increase your savings rate, when you don't see your savings growing as fast as you want.

- You will likely take on less risk, and earn a lower rate of return, as retirement age approaches because you fear losing what you've accumulated.

- Many recommended financial products prevent access to your money for years, with the pain of financial penalty if you want make a withdrawal.

- Predicting what will happen in the future is impossible. How many times have the financial experts been wrong? Very few forecast the depth of the recession of this last, or any, decade.

- What worked in the past is no guarantee that the same result will occur in the future.

The obstacles to accumulate money outside of your own motivation are numerous. Tax law changes, and some of the other obstacles, are shown in the following charts with a more detailed explanation in paragraph 6 below. We should add that most people are also susceptible to spending most, if not all of their income, and dip into their savings to spend more.

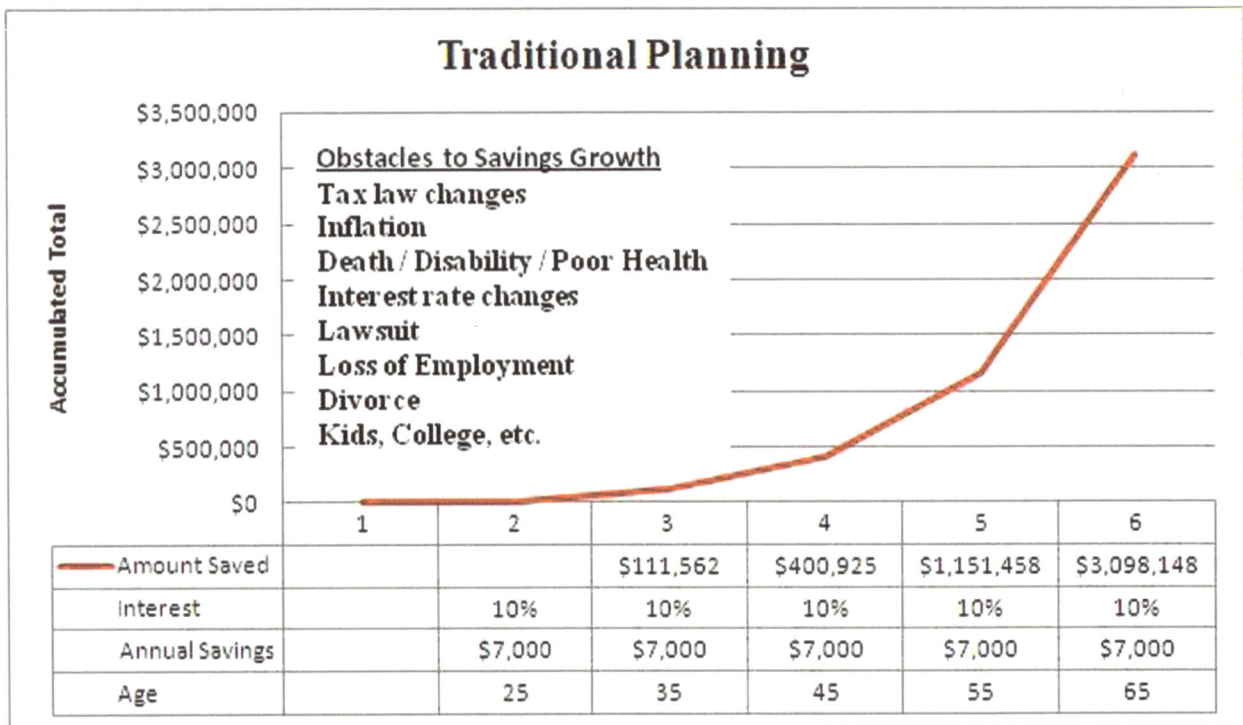

Traditional Planning

Obstacles to Savings Growth
Tax law changes
Inflation
Death / Disability / Poor Health
Interest rate changes
Lawsuit
Loss of Employment
Divorce
Kids, College, etc.

	1	2	3	4	5	6
Amount Saved			$111,562	$400,925	$1,151,458	$3,098,148
Interest		10%	10%	10%	10%	10%
Annual Savings		$7,000	$7,000	$7,000	$7,000	$7,000
Age		25	35	45	55	65

Looks good doesn't it? This is the picture that most financial firms will present to you as their planning process. The first problem is the constant interest rate. History shows that it is not realistic to expect a constant and stable rate of return on investments.

This picture provides a more realistic view, but what it really illustrates is that to get nearer the goal, the savings rate has to more than double because the interest rate is a little more realistic. This approach still mirrors needs planning.

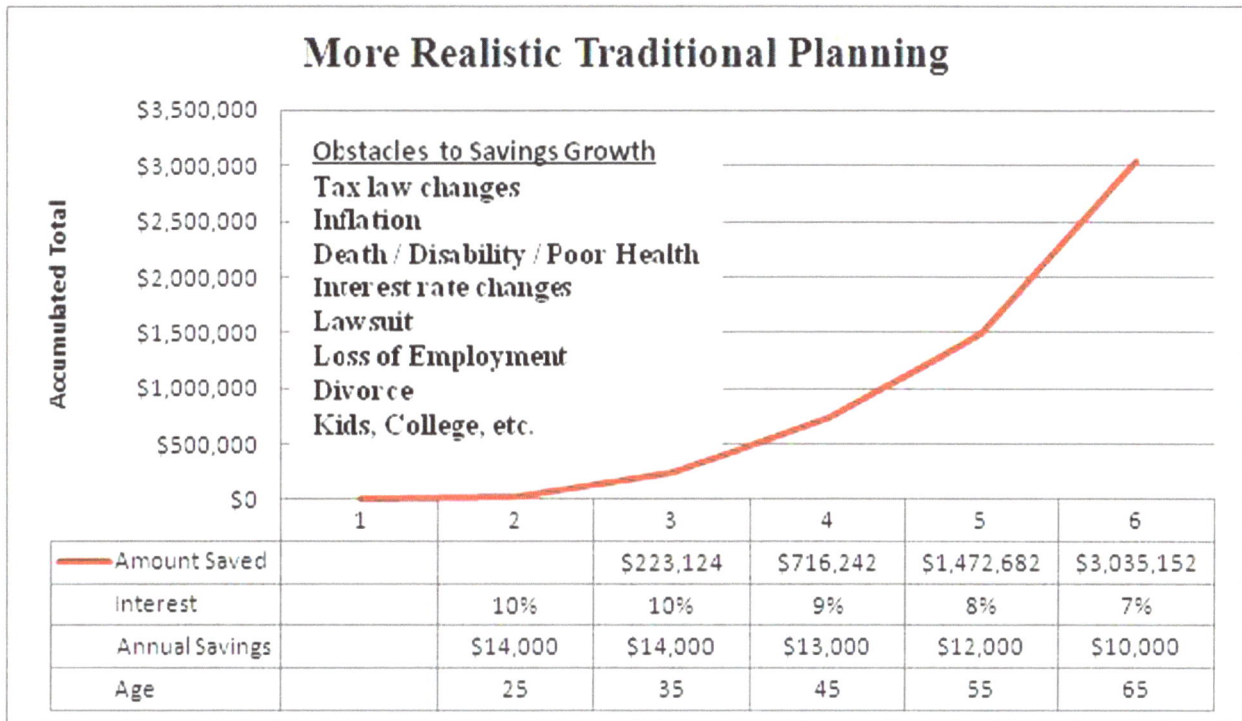

More Realistic Traditional Planning

	1	2	3	4	5	6
Amount Saved			$223,124	$716,242	$1,472,682	$3,035,152
Interest		10%	10%	9%	8%	7%
Annual Savings		$14,000	$14,000	$13,000	$12,000	$10,000
Age		25	35	45	55	65

Obstacles to Savings Growth
Tax law changes
Inflation
Death / Disability / Poor Health
Interest rate changes
Lawsuit
Loss of Employment
Divorce
Kids, College, etc.

6. Obstacle to savings growth

These are generally covered by a financial planner:

a) Market risk

Severe market downturns have occurred at least once in every decade since 1970, and are mostly unpredicted by the so-called financial experts, gurus, media pundits, and politicians.

- They ignored the big picture and concentrated on the smaller but more lucrative picture: making money for themselves through commissions, fees, and selling their own ideas through seminars, DVDs, and books.

- Corruption, collusion, and insider trading within financial institutions are causing billions of dollars lost to fraudulent dealing, and leave investors on the hook.

b) Tax law changes

How does any tax law change affect you?

- If tax rates go down, what do you do with any extra money?

- Conversely, should rates go up, what is the effect on your current financial strategies?

- For example, as of January 1, 2013 the payroll tax went back into effect. This effectively reduced your pay by 2%. What did you do? Did you continue to spend? Did you cut spending? Did you cut savings?

- This tax was originally cut during 2011 and 2012. This would have been a great time to have used the approximately $1,000 savings on a $50,000 annual income to increase your own savings. It's not just the federal taxes that increase. It's all the other taxes, too:

- State

- Sales

- Local government

- Estate

- Medicare

- Real estate

With the Affordable Care Act, or Obamacare, coming into full effect, the increases in the number of people qualifying for Medicaid, and the size of the federal deficit, you make the judgment on whether you believe taxes are going to increase or decrease in upcoming years.

c) Inflation

We don't necessarily see inflation in action, although we certainly feel its bite. Inflation is the increasing cost for the same item over years. The rate of inflation also varies by area. For example, New York may differ from Los Angeles.

Certainly the official rate of inflation has lessened considerably during the ten years ending in 2013, but costs certainly *seem* to be rising more rapidly than the index. For Example: Goods are repackaged to contain less product but sold at the same price.

Can you believe the government figures? Sometimes the CPI (Consumer Price Index) used doesn't include food and energy costs because they are considered "too volatile."

20 Year Inflation Graph, 1993 through 2013 [21]

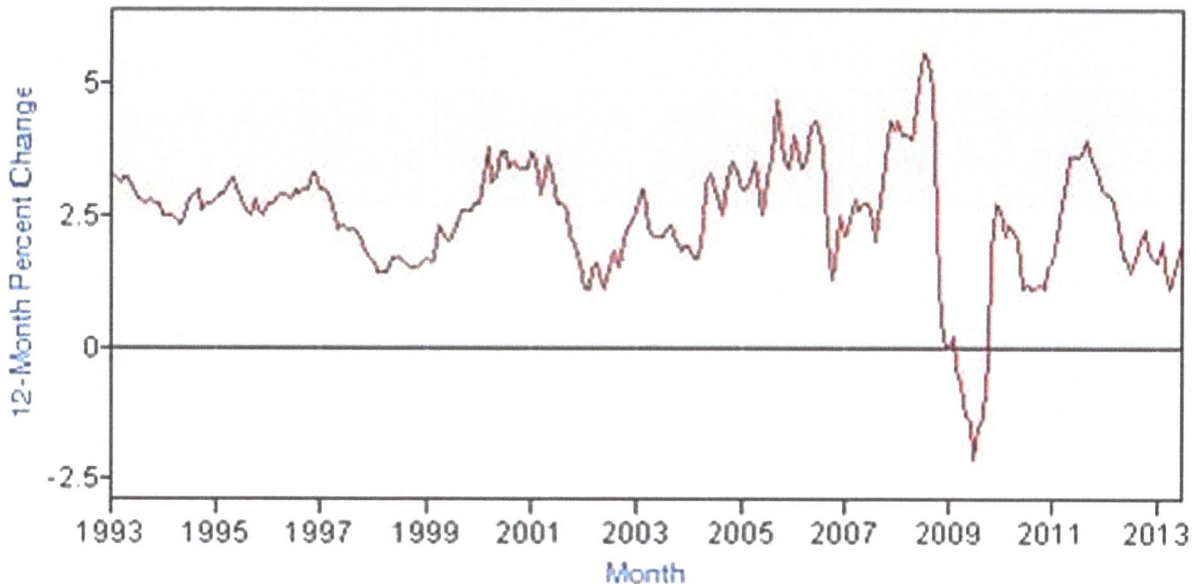

In many traditional plans, the following items are NOT accounted for:

d) Health or injury issues

How does your financial future look should you become sick, or suffer an injury, resulting in loss or reduction in pay?

e) Lawsuit

You're texting while driving and cause a serious accident with injuries. If you're sued and found at fault, how does your current financial plan work?

f) Death/Disability

Does your plan account for death or disability for you and your family?

g) Sickness of a family member

What happens to your finances when a family member becomes totally dependent on you for long-term care assistance?

h) Marriage/Divorce

Are you prepared for the cost of a wedding, which costs the average couple over $25,000? Over 50% of marriages end in divorce. Do you have, or need, a prenuptial agreement?

i) Beneficiaries

Are your beneficiaries named correctly and up to date on all legal documents?

---

[21] Source: Bureau of Labor Statistics: http://data.bls.gov/pdq/SurveyOutputServlet

j) Cash Reserves

Do you have sufficient reserves should you lose your job? Have you taken steps toward saving adequate liquid reserves while you are working?

k) Technological change

iPad, iPhone, plasma televisions, Kindle, Xbox, Windows XP, 7, 8 and 9, Droid, and sat navs are all technological must-haves that have come on the market within the last few years.

The pace of technological change means you will be spending ever-increasing sums of money just to keep a couple of steps behind progress. Then, better models become available every 6 months or so, and you must plan to catch up. The children's market has also increased the purchase of electronics exponentially.

The number one goal of your financial plan is to save a minimum of 15% of your gross income. This will help you offset the obstacles to your savings.

7. An alternative to traditional planning*

Our ultimate objective is to be happy with our lives. Start by focusing on goals and achievements that will further your progress toward increasing your happiness.
To do this, examine three areas with their respective goals:

a) Financial

Improve savings, wills, retirement plans, insurance, mutual and index funds.
This chapter is for planning finances but the principles also apply to personal and professional planning.

b) Personal

More time with spouse/partner children, lose/gain weight, regular exercise program, do charitable work, and hobbies.

c) Professional

Advance your career by studying for awards/grants/qualifications, join an organization/club for business contacts, lecture, write articles, author books, and other ways to move up the ladder.

Acknowledgement to Chuck McDowell, "The Financial Intelligence Experience" and Dan Sullivan "Strategic Coach."

8. The six step method to planning

I. Where am I today?

Knowing exactly where you stand today, gives you a starting line from which to measure your progress.

a) Consider each financial product that you have purchased over the years and determine the exact benefits you are receiving from them. What do they do for you, what do they not do for you, and why?

b) Don't be reluctant to face your financial situation because you are ashamed. This only makes small problems grow larger.

c) Accept your situation for what it is. Move on and start applying the **s.i.m.p.l.i.f.y.** philosophy to help get back on the right path.

II. Where do I want be in the future?

You have a limited amount of money passing through your hands in your lifetime which emphasizes the importance of saving, conserving, and maximizing the use of every dollar.

Although we can't predict the future financial performance of products, we can predict and compare ***their overall benefits*** to us over time.

For example:

- Are you getting tax benefits when making retirement contributions?
- Do you have easy access to your money for emergency purposes?
- While your accounts grow in value, are they growing tax free?
- Will you pay taxes when you take money out of the account?
- Are there any additional benefits paid if you become sick or injured?
- How does the product perform when I die?

Most people spend their time concentrating on the final dollar number that a product yields. It is a far better approach to concentrate on the bigger picture and look at the overall benefits you receive from a financial product.

III. How do I get there?

- Use short time frames, three to five years maximum.
- Predicting goals beyond even three years is difficult to visualize for most people.
- Solving financial problems is only part of the solution. Planning to take advantage of opportunities, and improving your strengths, is all part of the picture.
- List your financial opportunities, problems, and strengths. You may well end up with a large number of items on each list.
- You might find it advantageous to select the top three priorities and work on these first.
- As you complete the most important task, work on the next most important, and so on.
- Always ask yourself, "What is the next thing to do?" Your answer becomes your next action for which you should set a completion date.

IV. Who's going to help me?

Most people develop their professional representatives as the need arises, but it's a good idea to anticipate the experts you are likely to need and seek them out. Social media, especially LinkedIn for professional contacts, is playing a more important role in the selection process. Organizations such as Rotary, Chamber of Commerce, social and professional clubs, and fraternal organizations are also important places for meeting professionals on a personal basis.

These are the financial professionals you are likely to need at one time or another:

    a. Property and casualty insurance agent

    b. Life, disability, health insurance and annuities agent

    c. Financial Planner/Coach

    d. CPA

    e. Attorney

    f. Investment advisor to include stocks and bonds

    g. Residential real estate agent

    h. Commercial real estate agent

    i. Long-term care insurance agent

Some advisors may play multiple roles, but the sheer quantity and complexity of products, information, and misinformation prevents advisors from being competent in all areas.

V. How do I measure my progress?

Measure your progress by your goal achievement at, or within, the time limit you've specified. Change and improvement will likely be incremental rather than all at once.

    a) Be patient.

    b) Review regularly.

    c) Be consistent.

Consider making happiness with your progress toward achieving a goal as the measure of achievement.

VI. Taking action

Taking action is easier when you have someone helping you. This can be a family member, a professional, or a friend.

- A consistent, gentle nudge will keep you wanting to be on track.
- You may want to start with a review every three months and prepare to adjust the period to something that suits you, and your advisor, best.

Their advice should include:

- An analysis of the missed task and whether it should be your next priority.
- If it's not the next priority, where does it fit in your list of priorities?

Your financial decisions should act like a freeway. Maybe you're in the slow lane, maybe the fast lane, but at a minimum, you are headed in the right direction.

9. Finding the right financial advisor

This is an area where most people struggle. Entrusting your confidential financial information to a stranger or family friend/member is difficult. Recommendation was, and it still is, the best way to find an advisor.

- First you should seek expertise and competence because trust is earned over time.
- Despite the Bernie Madoffs of the world, the vast majority of the professionals you will meet are honest and trustworthy.
- Recommendations from family, colleagues, and friends offer sources, as do professional organizations.
- Professional qualifications show that the advisor has studied his chosen profession and qualified to use the designation in his title. Certified Financial Planner (CFP), Registered Investment Advisor (RIA) and others.
- Your chosen advisor and team should be able to answer any and all questions about the effect of chosen financial products and strategies on your life priorities, as well as your financial well being.
- Interview candidates personally and make sure they are people with whom you are comfortable.
- Don't allow yourself to be intimidated because you lack knowledge.
- Get references, and more importantly, talk to the references about the advisor's bad points as well as their good points.
- If something appears too good to be true, it probably is.

When did you last sit down with all of your advisors in one room? Answer: Never. This is not in your favor because it means your individual advisors may be unaware of your overall plan and their place within it.

Constructing your financial plan involves having a great team of advisors who implement a strategy approved by you. It works best when someone takes the role of quarterback to make sure your decisions are being implemented in the way the plan is laid out.

- The best person to be the quarterback is a competent financial advisor or coach.

Your financial advisor or coach's job is to assist you to:

- Construct and develop your financial strategies to achieve your priorities.
- Divide the strategies into the sub steps necessary to make the plan a success.
- Set up a time frame and deadline for the achievement of each strategy and sub step.
- Monitor progress through achievement of goals within the allocated timeline.
- Be non-judgmental.

Your choice of advisor should show expertise, experience, and knowledge when you are choosing financial products. Your advisor is best when unbiased. This is helped when the advisor doesn't earn compensation from commissions on sales of financial products you buy.

10. How financial advisors are compensated

The incentive plans offered by most financial companies encourages advisors on commission to sell products which pay them the best rate. The same product might not be best for you. A good advisor will sell you a product that works best for you, yet earns him/her less.

Your understanding of the product benefits is crucial, especially for the items in the contract which are out of your control, for example future cost increases, future interest rate increases, and others.

Financial advisors and coaches are compensated in one of four ways:

a) Fees with no commission earnings from product sales

b) Products sold earning a commission for the advisor

c) Fees and, with full disclosure, commissions from financial products you purchase

d) Fees for managing financial assets

Clearly a fee-only advisor is not pressured to sell you a highly-commissioned product but planning fees can be quite steep. Most financial companies and advisors will offer a free plan, or a substantial discount on fees, for people just entering the workplace.

- Any fee you pay for financial advice has lost its investment value forever. It's good to incorporate this value when taking account of the advice you are being given. In other words make sure you get a lot of bang for your buck.

- Financial coaches and advisors should be guides who help you achieve your full potential, with a plan which incorporates all of your priorities; financial, personal, and professional.

11. Your planning worksheet

Top 3 Financial Problems for Action				
Problem	**Strategy**	**Next Step**	**Due**	**Completed**
Poor financial record keeping	Have a paperless record keeping system	Create an Excel spreadsheet	11/1/2014	
Increase emergency savings	Save additional $100 monthly	Reduce restaurant meals and coffee purchases	10/1/2014	
Increase auto liability insurance coverage	Verify quantity of additional coverage needed	Call Phil at My Insurance Co. 310-555-1212 for	11/1/2014	
Top 3 Financial Opportunities for Action				
Opportunity	**Strategy**	**Next Step**	**Due**	**Completed**
Wealthy grandparents	Use gift from them to pay college loans	Arrange a meeting to discuss the possibilities	9/28/2014	
Obtain bonus for achieving sales goal at work	Contact 10 extra prospects a week to make 3 extra sales	Make a list of the likely prospects to call	10/1/2014	
Idea for a new pet business	Write a business plan	Research pet industry for competition	10/31/2014	
Top 3 Strengths for Improvement Action				
Strength	**Strategy**	**Next Step**	**Due**	**Completed**
Increase income	Work for promotion to management level	Take college class to improve expertise in people management	11/30/2014	
Considerable equity in home	Refinance and purchase rental property	Review rates and costs with a mortgage broker	11/31/2014	
Experienced in retail sales	Lecture at university	Make an appointment with the college dean	10/31/2014	

12. Software used in the financial industry

Software models are used throughout the financial industry to forecast your wealth accumulation values through retirement and even death. Be warned that the end numbers are not relevant when even reasonable assumptions are made. We cannot predict the future. However, the following programs simulate life circumstances and show how *product benefits* compare at their very core.

Leap Systems Inc.: www.leapsytems.com

Moneytrax: www.moneytrax.com

The Living Balance Sheet: www.thelivingbalancesheet.com

These software models are designed for use by financial professionals and not designed for use by the general public.

13. Planning for non-traditional and unmarried couples

The recent Supreme Court decision on DOMA (Defense of Marriage Act) now allows the federal government to acknowledge marriage between same sex couples but does not force states to follow the ruling. State laws vary, and marriage between same sex couples in one state may not be recognized under the laws of another.

In August 2013, the IRS announced that same sex couples who are legally married, no matter where, should file 2013 taxes as either "married filing jointly" or "married filing separately."

The ruling overrides any state law. The tax status of a same sex married couple when filing state tax returns, where the state does not recognize same sex marriage, remains unclear.

As of June, 2014, nineteen states recognize same sex marriage as legal. These decisions are by court decision, state legislature, and popular vote. Thirty-one states ban same sex marriages, most by constitutional amendment and state law.*
* http://gaymarriage.procon.org/view.resource.php?resourceID=004857

It should also be noted that many of these issues affect all domestic partners, heterosexual and LGBTcouples living together, and not just same sex couples.

Financial matters that can be affected include:

- Sale of a residence – exclusion of gain
- Passive loss limitations
- Income taxes on an individual versus married couple
- Medical and related benefits
- Cobra medical insurance premium subsidy
- Social Security benefits
- Qualified retirement plans
- Property transfers between domestic partners
- Wills and dying intestate (without a will)
- Healthcare proxies
- Unlimited gift tax marital deduction
- Unlimited estate tax deduction
- Gift splitting
- Tax on entire value of jointly-held property
- Workers compensation

Clearly, with the United States Supreme Court decision, the future of same sex marriage equality throughout the union is just a matter of time and lawsuit. However, until all the states fall into line, there will continue to be a difference between benefits provided to traditional married couples, couples living together and same sex married couples. These disparities detrimentally affect many financial areas unless the right planning is put in place.

It's very important to consult with a qualified legal advisor about your individual circumstances.

14. Why do I need a will, trust or a health directive?

a) Wills

You may think that you don't have much and it's not worth the bother, and you probably don't like to discuss death, but this is one of the most neglected areas of protection. Many of you have outdated and incorrect wills and trusts. Many of you just haven't bothered at all.

The real problem you create, by not having a will, is with the family members left behind. They have to deal with your belongings and may disagree on what you would have wanted. With technology today, it doesn't take long to create a will online. Your families will thank you for spelling out what you'd like done with your "stuff."

Having a will or not having a will has a similar effect:

- Decisions are court approved (probate) through a court appointee.
- Probate is a long and expensive process costing maybe 3 to 8% of the estate value.
- Probate can take a long time to settle, think months and years.
- There is no privacy for a court proceeding.
- If you have a will, the court will allocate your assets according to your wishes unless there is someone contesting the will or it's invalid.
- Without a will, a judge will be making decisions on your behalf.

Many people, including celebrities, lost large portions of their estates because they were inadequately protected.

b) Trusts

A trust is an arrangement under which one person, called a trustee, holds legal title to property for another person, called a beneficiary. You can be the trustee of your own living trust and keep full control over all property held in the trust.

A "living trust" (also called an "inter vivos" trust) is simply a trust created to be effective while you're alive, rather than one that is created at your death.

Among the benefits of having your estate held in a trust are:

- No court control which is very important if you become incapacitated and are no longer able to make decisions
- Avoids probate, as assets are distributed by your trustee according to your instructions
- Helps provide quicker asset distribution to beneficiaries
- Can help avoid estate taxes
- Little delay in the trust being executed

- There is no public record of your living trust details, so privacy is complete
- Easy to make changes and amendments or even cancel
- Much more difficult for others to contest
- Protects minors, dependents with needs
- You can structure a trust in almost any fashion to suit any need

c) Health Directive: Who turns off the machine when you're brain dead?

It is vital you complete a power of attorney directing your wishes should you lapse into a persistent vegetative state.

- Friends and family know their responsibilities and aren't stuck not knowing what you'd want.
- The Terri Schiavo case in Florida is a classic set of circumstances that need to be avoided at all costs.

Your circumstances can change from day to day. Review your wills and trusts every year or on a life-changing event to make sure they represent what you want to happen should something unexpected occur.

d) Don't forget your pets

A half million pets are killed each year because there was no plan to care for them when their owner had an unexpected illness, accident, or death.

15. Chapter Four: Highlights

- You must plan your finances because there is a limit to your lifetime income. Every dollar has to be conserved and used to its maximum efficiency.
- $75,000 annually gives you about $2,250,000 after-tax money with which to live, raise a family, save for retirement, pay college education, vacation, buy a home, as well as cover other expenses. Doesn't sound like too much, does it?
- There are three challenges to achieving your financial objectives: time and the pressure of everyday life, the sheer complexity and variety of financial choices, and taking action and the discipline required to do so.
- Start planning your finances NOW! Begin with a budget and save using two bank accounts. (See Chapter One: Savings)
- Make sure you have a good filing and record keeping system. (See Chapter One: Savings)
- The best plan would have a number of different attributes. Among them would be: regular contributions, a competitive return, tax-free contributions, growth and distributions, no penalties accessing your money, no loss of capital and minimum risk, protection from creditors, and provisions for death, disability, emergencies and unforeseen factors.
- You would control your plan, the government would not.

- Traditional planning focuses on questions such as the amount of money you need in retirement, the amount you're prepared to invest, and the amount of risk you would undertake.

- Traditional financial planning is flawed because it's based on planning for what you need, rather than maximizing the use of every dollar that comes into your possession.

- Traditional financial planning focuses on your future needs. Concentrate on focusing on financial, personal, and professional goals that will make you happier with your life.

- Don't assume everything will work out as you've planned.

- Don't use unrealistic or too optimistic of a rate of return on your investments. Understand that what happened in the past is an unreliable prediction of the future.

- When the market drops below your anticipated rate of return it has to work twice as hard to catch up.

- When you're missing your anticipated wealth accumulation targets, don't increase risk. Increase your savings instead.

- As you age and approach retirement you will want to take on less risk. Make sure you figure that in your calculations.

- The obstacles to savings growth are numerous. The top three covered by most advisors include: market risk, tax increases, and inflation.

- Don't forget that taxation is not just state and federal taxes. It also includes sales, local, government, estate, Medicare, and real estate taxes.

- Obstacles not generally covered when calculating savings growth include: health or injury issues, lawsuit losses, death, disability, marriage and divorce, and loss of employment.

- Technological change is a huge drain on financial resources especially when considering the children's market. The pace of change is extraordinary on items such as iPhones, iPods, plasma televisions, Kindles, Xbox, Droids, and others.

- An alternative to traditional planning would allow you to focus on furthering your progress and happiness in three areas of your life: financial, personal, and professional.

- There is a six-step method to planning. These steps include: Where am I today? Where do I want to be in the future? How do I get there? Who's going to help me? How do I measure my progress? And, taking action.

- Make a list of priorities, looking at opportunities, problems, and strengths in each part of your life; financial, personal, and professional. Work on the top three at any one time. Divide the priority into steps, each step leading toward the goal completion. Define each step by looking at the next task to accomplish that will bring the goal nearer to completion.

- Use short time frames and measure your progress by goal completion within the specified time frame.

- Get help where you can. It is not easy to plan, and having a coach or guide will not only help structure a plan, but also give you the reinforcement you need to execute it.

- Build a team of advisors around you who are experts in law, real estate, insurance, and other areas. Your coach or guide should coordinate your strategies by being a quarterback who communicates your requirements to each expert and follows up to ensure completion.

- Finding the right advisor is not easy because you are handing over your confidential financial information. First seek out expertise and competence. Trust is earned over time.

- Recommendation is still the best way to find a financial advisor.

- Professional qualifications are certainly an indication that the advisor has studied their business and qualified for certain designations.

- Interview candidates personally and check references carefully.

- If something about a financial product or strategy seems too good to be true, it probably is.

- Financial advisors are compensated in a number of different ways. Financial companies encourage advisors to sell specific products by offering increased commissions on those products. Make sure the product benefits you in the way that's best for you and your financial goals.

- Advisors who earn a fee for creating your plan and strategies, while not earning a commission on product sales, are probably the least biased of any advisor.

- Each financial company has its own financial software analysis program. Most of these are designed for use by professional advisors rather than the general public. Look for software that illustrates product benefit comparisons rather than just wealth accumulation.

- Planning for same sex and unmarried couples can be complex. The federal government now acknowledges marriage between same sex couples but does not force states to follow the ruling. State laws vary and what is recognized by one state may not be recognized by another.

- The IRS has advised same sex couples who are legally married, no matter which state they reside in, to file "married filing jointly" or "married filing separately." This ruling overrides state law, but filing state returns where the state does not recognize same sex marriage remains unclear.

- Same sex marriage and couples living together, heterosexual and LGBT, are affected by many financial matters including taxes, health insurance, retirement benefits, property transfers, wills, and many other areas. The living together approach is not being married and treated as two single individuals when being treated as being married would make a financial difference. These differences have to be accounted for in a serious long term relationship.

- It is very important to consult with a qualified legal advisor about your individual circumstances.

- It seems inevitable that all states will eventually recognize same sex marriage and allow the same benefits as a conventional marriage.

- Many of you have outdated and incorrect wills and trusts. Many of you have not bothered to prepare for the time when you are no longer alive. Unfortunately, the burden caused by such lack of preparation falls on the people left behind who often disagree on what you would have wanted.

- Probate is the process by which the property of someone who dies, either with a will or without, is distributed. In other words, a judge makes the final decision although the judge will certainly comply with your wishes if you have a will unless it is invalid or contested.

- Probate can be an extremely long and expensive process which is public and therefore not private.

- Trusts are many and varied, but are generally a more efficient way of transferring assets than a will. You can be the trustee of your own trust and thus retain full control of the assets. A living trust is one intended to be used while you are alive rather than at death.

- There are many benefits to having a trust; no court control, avoids probate, and quicker distribution to beneficiaries, are amongst those benefits. There is no public record which assists with privacy, and changes are easy to make. You can structure a trust to accomplish almost whatever you want.

- One of the most common errors with respect to trusts is failing to fund the trust with the assets you intend to protect. Another is failing to adjust the trust, especially with regards to the beneficiaries, as your life circumstances change.

- Having a health directive is very important. This is a power of attorney directing your wishes when you lapse into a vegetative state.

- Don't forget your pets. A half million pets are killed each year because their owner had made no provision for when they died or could no longer look after the pet.

chapter five:
l is for learning

BALANCE COLLEGE DEBT AGAINST POTENTIAL CAREER EARNINGS.

Chapter Five focuses on learning. Descriptions are provided for informational purposes only. Everyone's financial situation is different, and financial purchases should be tailored to the individual. There are no recommendations to purchase products from any particular company. You are strongly advised to consult with experts and licensed professionals as well as to seek legal and accounting advice, before making your financial decisions.

1. Going to college

a) What's wrong with this picture?

Today, the ever-increasing cost of a college education is putting a damper on college plans with many college educations costing over $100,000. The lenders, especially the federal government, are being repaid, the universities are charging higher and higher fees and getting paid, generous salaries and benefits for faculty members are getting paid. The students and their families are footing the bill.

Repaying college loans has become a drag on the future spending power, and life goals, of many graduates. While college loans are being repaid; houses, autos, and household goods are not being purchased, resulting in a highly negative effect on the economy as a whole.

President O'Bama has signed an executive order to be in effect in December, 2014 which affects loans taken between October, 2007 and October, 2011 at 10% of discretionary income. Unfortunately, this order only affects Pay as You Earn loans which are a very small percentage of student loans.

b) Career earnings versus cost of degree

Whatever your intended occupation and the degree needed, the first step should be calculating your potential earnings versus the cost of college education. It makes no sense to encumber yourself with tremendous debt, when your chosen career offers poor salary expectations. It's asking for trouble because it will be a huge drain on your resources for many years.

Knowing your lifetime earnings is critical to happiness and financial success. (Also see Chapter One: Savings, and Chapter Four: Planning)

As with all areas of finance, the rules change frequently, and what information is good today may not be good tomorrow. Unless there are some changes, it is clear that going to college is going to remain an expensive proposition.

Figure 3
Work-Life Earnings of Bachelor's Degree Holders by College Major

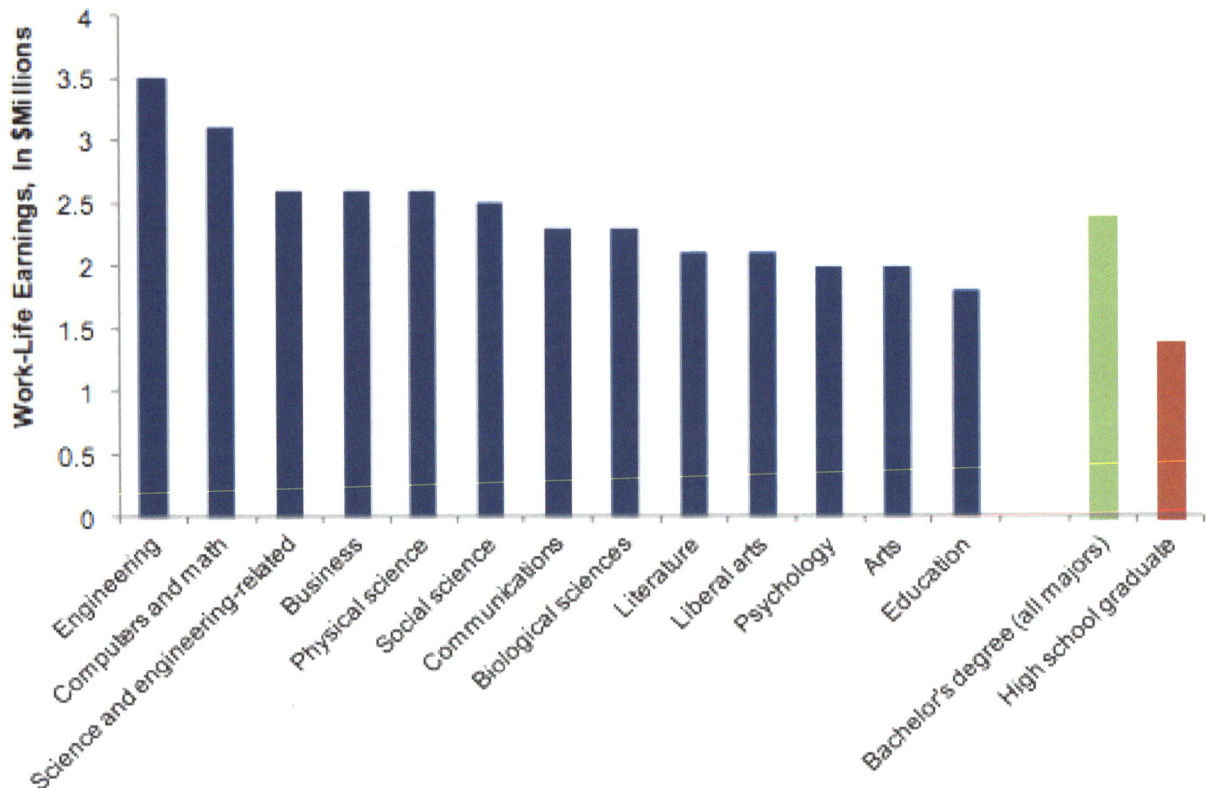

Source: Julian (2012).
Note: Synthetic work-life earnings estimates are calculated by finding median earnings for each 5-year age group between 25 and 64 (25-29, 30-34, etc.). Earnings for each group is multiplied by 5 to get total earnings for that period, then aggregated to get total lifetime earnings. This is done for high school graduates, bachelor's degree holders, and bachelor's degree holders by major.

22

---

[22] Source: Tiffany Julian, Census Bureau, October 2012

- While a degree will not guarantee employment, you are more likely to be employed than someone without a degree.

- After five consecutive years of belt tightening, some states are increasing higher education budgets as their financial picture improves.

c) Lower education costs in the future?

Future education cost reduction will probably come with technology and the internet, with technological improvements already playing an increasing role. The cost savings for the student will make this type of learning delivery very attractive. It will also be a motivator for higher learning institutions to lower costs.

Currently, until the hiring culture changes, recruiters are more likely to feel that an online degree is not as credible as attending a brick and mortar college. Recruiters hiring decisions are still often based on the reputation of the school attended.

d) Don't discount the "experience" benefit of a higher education

It's not just about getting a degree leading to your career, it's also about the life experience:

- You can develop your abilities in an academic world under the direction of mentors and professors who are expert in the subjects you study and/or have interest.

- A social setting, where you're often living away from home for the first time, helps you understand "real life" outside of your parent's protection.

- Maximizes your ability to make connections, network, and create opportunities

e) Junior colleges

Never underestimate the value of attending a community college for two years before going on to a four-year college program. As you mature you will begin to view the world in a wider light which opens up your mind to fresh opportunities. For more information see Chapter Four: Planning

f) The relationship between level of education, average earnings, and unemployment

- College graduates are more likely to be employed than someone with only a high school diploma.

- You are likely to earn more too. An Associate's degree will bring you a 30% higher income than those who just graduate high school, while those with a Bachelors degree typically earn 75% more.

23

Why go to college? Can't I get a good job now?
Yes, maybe you could, but a college degree will make your chances even better. Check out the earnings and unemployment rates for people 25 years and older with different levels of education:

	Less than a high school diploma	High school graduate, no college	Some college, no degree	Occupational program (career school)	Associate degree (academic program)	Bachelor's degree	Master's degree	Doctoral degree (e.g., Ph.D.)	Professional degree (e.g., M.D., J.D.)
Mean (average) earnings in 2011	$29,848	$41,288	$46,228	$49,920	$52,988	$71,552	$84,448	$102,648	$121,212
Unemployment rate in 2011	14.1%	9.4%	8.7%	6.6%	6.9%	4.9%	3.6%	2.5%	2.4%

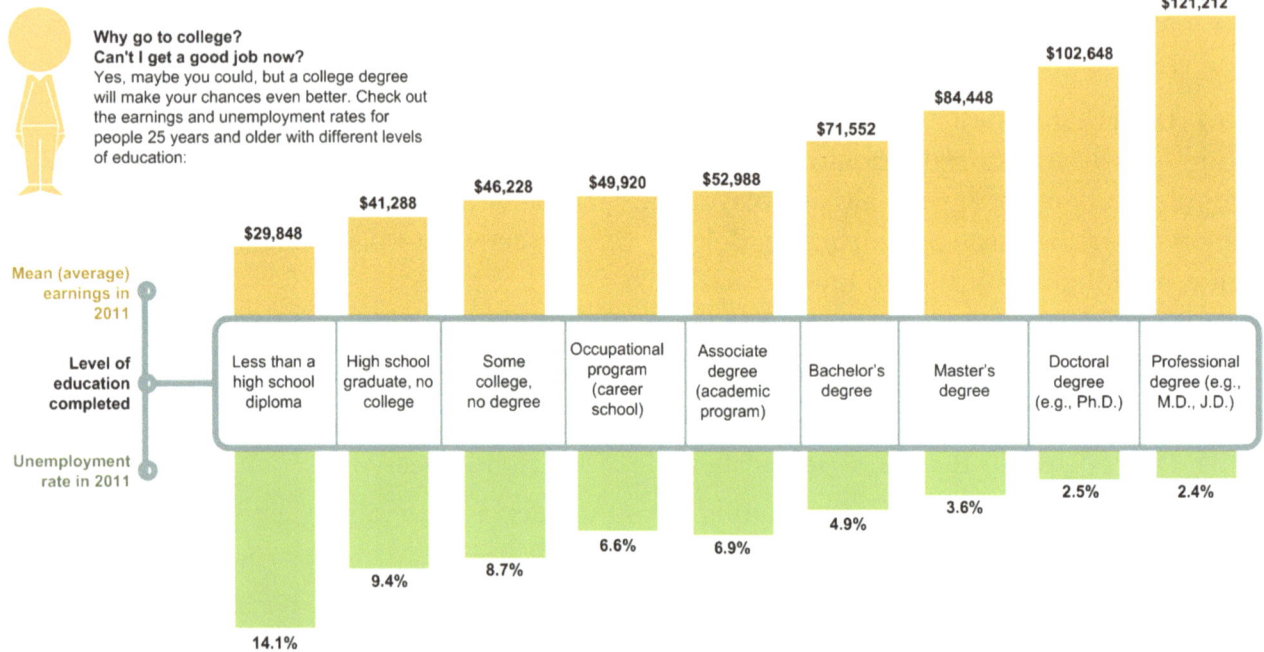

Source: Bureau of Labor Statistics, Current Population Survey, unpublished tables, 2012.

2. Some reasons education costs are increasing

Education costs have typically been higher than the normal rate of inflation. In 2011 they were running at about 6%. When costs rise, to a great extent, that cost is passed on to you. Here are several reasons costs are rising:

- High salaries and pension rights: To attract the best, high salaries are offered to college professors and administrators. Their retirement payouts are equally very generous and sometimes guaranteed.

- Demand: Large numbers of students applying for a limited number of spaces equals higher costs.

- Upgrading of facilities: Academic, research, living, recreational, and technology have to be continually upgraded to compete.

- Other: Dorm costs, cafeteria expense, and security all incur extra costs which are nibbling away at the university budget.

---

[23] Source: Graphic Created by Visal.ly, http://visual.ly/why-go-college

24

Tuition and Fees 2013 Dollars

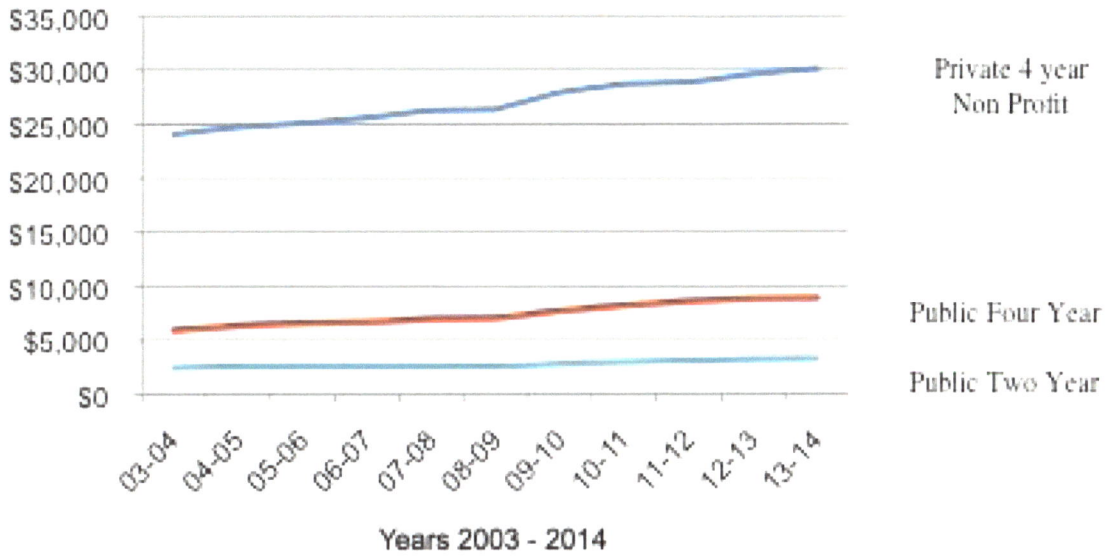

Private 4 year
Non Profit

Public Four Year

Public Two Year

Years 2003 - 2014

Tuition, Fees, Room and Board 2013 Dollars

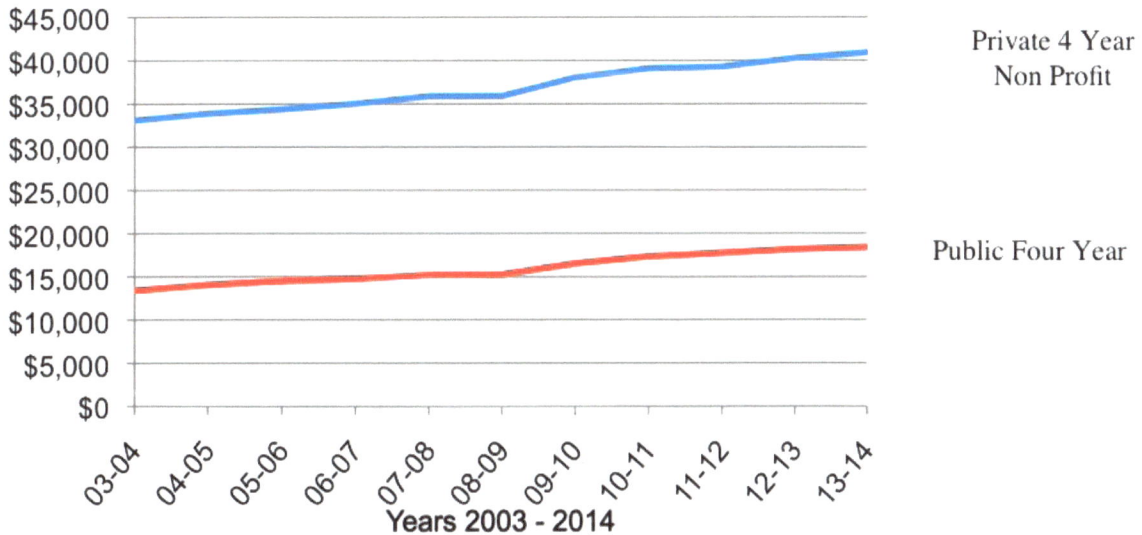

Private 4 Year
Non Profit

Public Four Year

Years 2003 - 2014

---

[24] *Source: The College Board, Annual Survey of Colleges; NCES, IPEDS: October 2013*

3. Is going to college worth the financial commitment?

Yes, college graduates can earn at least 30% more than those without a degree, but the increasing costs means a diminishing return on your investment. It is very important to consider the long-term effects of the cost of college on your financial future.

- You should determine the balance between college debt and potential earnings in your chosen field. Understand the entry, mid-level and the upper-level earnings potential for your chosen profession, and borrow the least amount of money possible to finance your degree

- Think of your college education as an investment. You want to obtain as high a rate of return on that investment as you can.

- Take into account the value of the college experience.

- Educate yourself about financial matters early in life.

- Make sure that when you graduate you know how to organize yourself financially. (See Chapters One: Savings and Four: Planning)

- Defaulting on loans even through bankruptcy is not an option: College loans have to be repaid.

- Understand the impact of your monthly education loan payments on your financial life before taking the loan.

- Spending more on an education than your earnings are likely to justify, is poor planning.

Education provides a reinforcement of a student's skills to successfully work in their chosen field. Very little weight is given to the importance of how they will deal with their earnings. To be successful requires knowledge of how money works. Generally, universities and colleges offer woefully inadequate education in this area.

4. Four steps to calculate the cost of your college education

Step 1: Expected family contribution
This is a calculation of the minimum amount expected of a student to pay toward the cost of higher education. You start the process with completion of two financial aid forms:

The Free Application for Federal Student Aid (FAFSA): Students must complete this application to determine eligibility for federal and state aid.

Many private colleges also require a College Scholarship Service (CSS) Application using the PROFILE form.

- Submit forms online.

- Analysis by a processing center will supply a minimum amount you will be expected to contribute. The analysis includes the assets and income of parents, benefits, family size, and other dependent children in college.

- Recent tax returns, financial statements, and other supporting documentation will also be required.

- Very few students qualify for complete financial aid, so nearly all students will have out-of-pocket costs.

- Most colleges will have a calculator on their website so you can readily get an approximate cost of attending that college.

Step 2: The cost of college
Calculate the total cost of attendance at college including; tuition, fees, room and board, enrollment, and other expenses.

Step 3: Calculate the difference
If your expected family contribution is less than the cost of college, you may qualify for financial aid in the form of scholarships and grants. If your expected family contribution is more than the cost of college, you will have to fill the financial gap personally, normally with student loans.

Step 4: Calculate net cost

Cost of college (tuition, housing, books, transportation, and other expenses)

Minus

Financial aid (: scholarships, grants, state grants, Pell grants)

Equals

Net cost of college

5. Saving for a college education

a) Having a college savings account is important
The importance of saving for a college education is shown in studies demonstrating that students with less than $500 in an account dedicated to college savings are three times more likely to enroll and 4.5 times more likely to graduate than a student with no savings. It is also suggested that having even having a small amount of savings dedicated to college, may better prepare students academically for the rigors of college.[25]

There are a number of ways of saving for your college education. Remember that the rules are constantly changing so you must check the current status from a federal and state perspective to suit your individual situation. The following are the most common:

b) The 529 Plan
A 529 Plan is designed to encourage savings for a higher education. Contributions are made to the fund on behalf of a beneficiary, usually a child or grandchild. Establishing a 529 Plan is an investment decision where each state structures its own plan with different investment options.

---

[25] *William Elliott, Hyun-a Song, Ilsung Nam, Center for Social Development, Research Brief, March 2013*

There are two kinds of 529 Plans which differ according to your state.

1. 529 Prepaid Tuition Plan:

This plan is only offered by a very limited number of states. You are buying tuition at today's prices, and the state assumes the risk for tuition increases providing you attend an in-state school. It's possible to also include room and board. There are generally age restrictions on the beneficiary.

2. 529 College Savings Plan:

This plan is currently offered by nearly all states. The fund is an investment account, often mutual funds, and subject to market variation.

Financial institutions are generating millions of dollars in fees, commissions and earnings as the total investment by American families in 529 Plans has now reached a record level of $190.7 billion. [26]

Contributions by way of gift were limited in 2014 to $14,000 per year, per contributor. Otherwise the contributor may incur taxes. A lump sum of $70,000 per contributor can be contributed, providing the gift is reported over five years. You can only gift cash, no stocks, bonds, or other financial instruments.

- Total balance in a 529 Plan has a lifetime limit up to $320,000 but there can be state variations on annual limits.

- These plans are not insured by the Federal Deposit Insurance Corporation (FDIC) except in four states where the underlying investment fund is invested in Certificates of Deposit (CDs).

- States set a limit on the total amount that can be contributed to any one account. Limits vary by state.

- Funds grow free of federal taxes and often free of state taxes too. Check your individual state.

- Withdrawals are tax free, providing they are used for qualified higher education expenses by the beneficiary. This includes tuition, books, fees, and room and board.

- Tax free withdrawal by the beneficiary now includes computers, printers, and software.

- There is no federal tax deduction for the person making the contribution, but there may be a state deduction.

- States may make it more advantageous to attend a higher-learning institution within the state by offering financial incentives. This can include tax deductions, grants, and scholarships. Check your individual state.

- The funds within a 529 Plan can be used at almost any accredited US college or university.

- The 529 Plan is an investment account, and fees and management expenses are charged. Make sure they're not excessive.

---

[26] *The College Savings Plans Network's (CSPN) 529 Report March 2013*

- Your investment account choice is limited to those offered by your state's plan. However, you may be able to change the type of investment account on an annual basis. Prepaid accounts offer no choice of investment account type.

- You should set up a separate 529 Plan fund for each beneficiary.

c) Disadvantages of the using the 529 Plan

The financial institutions have done a great job marketing the 529 Plan as a way to save for college. Once again, they get your money under control for long periods of time to use it to earn money before they have to give it back. The disadvantages of a 529 Plan are either downplayed or remain unmentioned. They include:

- The money in a 529 Plan, whether owned by a parent, grandparent, or a student will count as a parental asset when applying for student aid.

- The difference between the cost of education, and what you could have made through investing the contributions yourself, is the true cost of college.

- No accounting for children obtaining grants, scholarships, or other sources of money. It's possible their college education could be free. You might be stuck with an education savings account you no longer need and can only access with penalty.

- There are no guarantees of return of your money in the event of a financial failure, and it is possible to lose money.

- State and federal taxes, as well as penalties, cause distributions used for other than education expenses to be highly expensive.

- Limitations on choice of investment and ability to make timely changes

- Limitation on contribution amounts

- Distributions to pre-college (K through12) education expenses are not qualified.

d) Coverdell ESA

This is a similar plan to a 529 Plan and has many of the same disadvantages. It covers qualified education expenses with the same tax advantages, but with a much lower contribution allowance.

- The annual contribution limit is $2,000

- The contribution is adjusted down according to your income, with higher earners losing the ability to make a contribution at all.

- You cannot make a contribution to a Coverdell ESA after the beneficiary reaches 18 years old, unless the child has special needs. This prevents a contribution when the beneficiary has enrolled in a college.

- Distribution, unlike the 529 Plan, is mandatory within 30 days after the beneficiary turns age 30. The beneficiary would then pay state and federal taxes, as well as penalties, on the distribution.

- You are permitted to rollover your account once per year naming either the same, or a different, beneficiary without tax or penalty.

- You can rollover your plan once per year, without changing beneficiaries, to change investment options without penalty.

- There is no gift tax concern because the contribution limit is $2,000 - well below the annual gift limit of $14,000 for 2014.

It's permitted to have both a Coverdell ESA and a 529 Plan for the same beneficiary. If someone other than the student remains the account owner, the account will not be classified as a student asset. Distributions from either plan are not classified as student income. Both of these points are advantageous in terms of obtaining student aid.

6. Paying for a college education

As shown in the chart, college costs are rising faster than family income, making a college education more unaffordable.

a) College costs and median family income[27]

College costs and median family income, 1982 to 2012

Inflation-adjusted increases

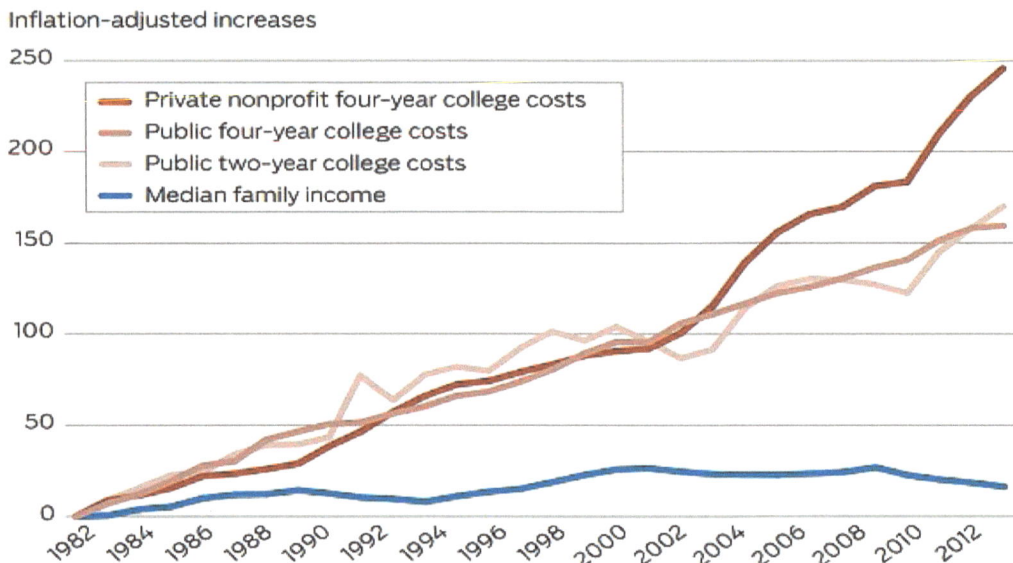

Sources: The College Board, Annual Survey of Colleges; National Center for Education Statistics, Integrated Postsecondary Education and Data System.

Note: Data is for persons age 25 and over. Earnings are for full-time wage and salary workers. These education categories reflect only the highest level of education attained. They do not take into account completion of training programs in the form of apprenticeships and other on-the-job training, which may also influence earnings and unemployment rates.

---

27 Source: Bureau of Labor Statistics, Current Population Survey.

b) The economic picture is gloomy

If you dwell on all of the bad news that surrounds you, mostly from news media hype, there are all kinds of statistics that you can use to prove your case. It's mostly stuff you cannot do anything about so relegate it to the waste bin. Forget about the bad news, and go out and make your own good news. Anything is possible and opportunity knocks often. Learn to recognize and act on those opportunities to help achieve your life priorities. Deals are made in any economy.

7. There are many ways to fund your college education

Higher education is normally paid for through a number of different avenues. There are innumerable online sites which describe the various methods you can use to pay for your higher education. They generally fall into the following categories:

- Using the savings plans already outlined above
- College Aid: Scholarships and grants
- Stafford Loans
- Pell Grants
- Perkins Loans
- Direct Loans
- Student Loans
- Federal Work-Study Programs

You're going to get a good estimate of your costs by visiting the college websites of those schools you want to attend.

8. Scholarships and grants

The big advantage with scholarships and grants is that they do not have to be repaid. This means that you are not incurring interest on loans. Consequently, you should be applying for as many as possible, especially grants as many go unfunded each year.

a) Pell Grants

Federal Pell Grants usually are awarded only to undergraduate students who have not earned a bachelor's or a professional degree yet and are financially needy.

- A Pell Grant amount may vary year to year. It does not have to be repaid. For the year ending June 2015, the maximum grant amount is $5,730.

b) Perkins Loan

This program offers low interest loans to the neediest of students. These loans are obtained directly from one of about 1,700 participating higher education facilities, although the funding is subsidized from the federal level.

- There are both annual and total loan limits, currently $5,500 and $27,000. The loan rate is currently fixed at 5% and the repayment period is up to 10 years.

c) Federal Work-Study (FSA) Program

This is a way to earn money and reduce the amount you are borrowing to pay for your education.

- You must qualify by way of financial need.
- Both undergraduates and graduates may qualify for part-timework both on and off campus.
- Programs emphasize employment in civic education or your course of study.
- Earnings are at least the federal minimum wage where undergraduates are compensated hourly, whereas graduates or professional students may be compensated by the hour or with salary.
- You will be paid directly by the school at least once a month.

9. College Loans

These fall into two groups, government and privately funded.

- You can deduct the interest paid on a student loan up to a limit of $2,500.
- It's possible to obtain more than one type of student loan if eligibility is met.

a) Deferment

Under certain terms and conditions such as unemployment, economic hardship, or health problems, a student may be unable to repay their federal student loan. They may qualify for deferment, meaning the interest on the loan is subsidized by the federal government during the period. The interest may be added to the loan principle.

b) Forbearance

The same type of circumstances as with deferment; unemployment, economic hardship or health problems, except the interest continues to accumulate and the student is responsible for paying it.

c) Grace period

Generally you are not required to start loan payments until six months after graduation, sometimes nine months. This might allow you to settle into life after college with a job before you start having to repay your loans.

10. Stafford or Direct Loans (government loans)

The Federal Direct Loan program is administered by the Department of Education, and offers low interest loans to students. These are broad outlines of the programs, and more research will be needed by you to determine your eligibility and qualification.

a) Direct Subsidized Loans

- For undergraduates and based on student need
- You have to be enrolled for at least half time in a degree program.
- No interest charged during time at school or deferment period

- Loans funded between July 1, 2012 and July 1, 2014 will be charged interest during the grace period which left unpaid will accumulate to the loan principal.

- Payments do not start until six months after graduation or leaving college.

b) Direct Unsubsidized Loans

- For undergraduates: Since July 2012 graduate and professional students are no longer permitted to take part in this program.

- Qualification for student need is not a requirement.

- In July 2013 a limit, the "maximum eligibility period" was introduced. Briefly, Direct Unsubsidized loans only will be available for up to 150% of the published length of the program.

- Interest is charged from the date the loan is funded.

- Although payments can be delayed until six months after graduation, the loan interest accumulates (accrues) to the loan balance. Meaning you pay more.

c) Direct PLUS Loans

This is an unsubsidized loan for parents of dependent students, and graduate or professional degree students. Good credit is important. Loan fees, not interest rates, are 4.204% of the amount borrowed.

d) Direct Consolidation Loans

Eligible federal student loans can be consolidated into one loan.

e) Loan amounts

Both subsidized and total loan amounts are limited depending on whether you are a dependent or independent student, and whether your parents qualify for a Direct Plus Loan. Loan amounts are also limited in both the total amount of loans borrowed, and the amount of both subsidized and unsubsidized loan amounts

f) Interest Rates

For loans taken after July 2013 the rules have changed, interest is now a variable rate linked to the bond equivalent rate of a 10-year treasury bill auctioned the previous June 1, plus a surcharge as follows:

In June 2014 the rate on the 10 year bill was an increase over the previous year going from 1.81% to 2.61%. This effectively raised the interest rate on all loans by 0.8% taken after July 1, 2014 through July 1, 2015.

- Federal Direct Subsidized Stafford Loans, for undergraduates.
  Rate is (2.61%) plus 2.05%. For 2014-2015 the interest rate will be 4.66%.

- Federal Direct Subsidized Loans for undergraduates:
  Rate is 2.61% plus 2.05%. For 2014-2015 the interest rate will be 4.66%

- Federal Direct Unsubsidized Loans for graduate and professional students:
  Rate is 2.61% plus 3.6%. For 2014-2015 the interest rate will be 6.21%

- Federal Direct PLUS Loans for parents of dependent students, and graduate or professional degree students. Rate is 2.61% plus 4.6%. For 2014-2015 the interest rate will be 7.21%.

- These rates will then be fixed for the duration of the loan. Rates will be published on or before June 5 of the year preceding.

- Consolidated Loans: Interest rate to be the *lesser* of the weighted average of the loans consolidated, or 8.25% being the maximum amount of interest that can be charged.

11. Repayment options on federal loans

Generally these fall into a number of categories each with different options. Not all repayment options are available for every loan. Terms and conditions do change, so you should contact your loan servicer to find out which option is best for you.

a) Find a repayment option to suit your budget:
  i. **Standard:** Fixed monthly payment up to a 10-year repayment period.
  ii. **Graduated:** Monthly payments are lower at first and increase over time up to a 10-year repayment period.
  iii. **Extended:** Payments may be fixed or graduated over a repayment period up to 25 years.
  iv. **Income based:** A maximum of 15% of your discretionary income (the difference between your adjusted gross income and 150% of the poverty guideline for your state). Repayment period is up to 25 years when the remaining balance is forgiven.
  v. **Pay as you earn:** A maximum of 10% of your discretionary income (the difference between your adjusted gross income and 150% of the poverty guideline for your state). Repayment period up to 20 years
  vi. **Income contingent:** Payments are calculated based on your adjusted gross income and the amount of your Direct Loans. Repayment period up to 25 years.
  vii. **Income sensitive:** Your monthly payment is based on your annual income. Repayment period up to 10 years.

12. Student loans from non-federal sources

It may be that you have to draw a loan from conventional lenders rather than the federal government to fund your college tuition. This is where the fundamentals take over and it is vital you understand the cost of borrowing versus your earning capability. Paying off college loans, and having little money to enjoy and progress in life otherwise, makes for a heavy burden.

- States: Most states offer loan programs.
- Colleges: Many colleges have their own loan programs.

- Financial institutions· This is the second largest lender for student loans after the federal government.

a) Repayment options on non-federal student loans

You should maximize the amount of federal loans available to you before seeking out institutional loans. In this way you make sure that you have maximum flexibility in your repayment program.

Repaying an institutional lender offers a mixed bag of terms and conditions depending on the lender. Most offer a variable rate linked to an index, either LIBOR or the Prime Rate, and some offer a fixed rate. These loans are not guaranteed by the federal government so default means the lender is on the hook.

- Institutional lenders do not generally offer deferment of loan payments or interest. Under certain conditions they will offer forbearance.

- Having a credit worthy co-signer is a plus and may even cause your loan interest to be discounted. The co-signer guarantees payment on the loan and will have to repay it should you fail to repay the loan.

There is always the opportunity to attend a community college for two years before transferring to a four-year school. This would be a good way to cut down on the amount of loans you need to pay for your education.

13. Defaulting on your college loans

Student loan debt is the only form of consumer debt that has grown since the peak of consumer debt in 2008. Balances of student loans have eclipsed both auto loans and credit cards, making student loan debt the largest form of consumer debt outside of mortgages.

Delinquency in all age groups is up. They show students under the age of 30 are currently experiencing an 8.9% rate, and this percentage grows enormously with age. Those in the 40 – 49 age groups show a 16.1% delinquency rate.[28]

a) Defaulting on a federal student loan

- The entire loan balance becomes due and payable immediately.

- You lose eligibility for more federal student aid, deferment, forbearance, and repayment plans.

- A collection agency will be assigned to your account.

- Credit bureaus will be notified affecting your credit rating, meaning house, car, and other purchases may be denied, or obtainable only at a very high interest rate.

- State and federal tax refunds may be taken and applied to the defaulted loan.

- Your wages or salary may be garnished by your employer.

- Federal employees risk losing 15% to garnishment.

---

[28] *Source: Federal Reserve Bank of New York, 2012 figures released March 29, 2013*

- There is a risk of legal action tying up assets and causing large associated fees.
- Bankruptcy is not automatic and only granted when undue hardship is found.

b) Defaulting on a conventional student loan

- Recourse is by way of obtaining a judgment through legal action.
- Bankruptcy is not an option unless you can show undue hardship.
- Wages can be garnished to satisfy the judgment.
- A levy (charge) can be made on your financial assets.
- A lien can be placed against your property.
- Credit bureaus and collection agencies will be notified, resulting in poor credit ratings affecting borrowing power and interest rates.

c) Cancellation/Forgiveness

Under certain terms and conditions some federal student loans can be forgiven, cancelled, or reduced. You will have to research your individual situation to find out the terms under which you may be qualified.

For example, public service employees who have paid and are current under their Direct Loans for a period of 10 years will have the remainder of their loan forgiven.

14. Using retirement savings to pay for college education

a) IRAs and Roth IRAs

You can make a withdrawal from an IRA and a Roth IRA to pay for qualified higher education costs. Providing the withdrawal does not exceed the cost for higher education there will be no tax or penalty. You cannot use either IRA to pay off old college loans.

b) 401(k)s

These plans should be rolled over into an IRA before education costs can be paid without penalty or tax.

There are hardship rules which allow you to pay for the following 12 months of higher education costs providing you meet all the requirements. However, you will have to pay taxes and penalties if you are under 59 ½.

Bear in mind, when calculating any additional tax for both IRAs and 401(k)s, the IRS requires the qualified educational costs to be reduced by any tax-free educational assistance such as Pell Grants, veteran's benefits, employer provided assistance, and scholarships.

c) Paying for your child's college education and its effect on retirement savings

Most parent worry about how their kids will afford a college education but most will help financially if they are able. One important consideration is the effect of helping pay for a college education with retirement savings.

In the example below, we show the loss in the retirement account when a contribution is made to help with a child's education. $10,000 which would normally be allocated to the retirement account is diverted to help with college costs for a period of only five years. The effect on the retirement account is devastating. Taking out just $10,000 per year for five years reduces your retirement account by nearly $100,000 by age 65.

Contribution for 40 years				
	Start Age	End Age		
Contribution Years	20	65	40	Years
Contribution Amount			$ (10,000.00)	
Interest Rate			4.00%	
Total at age 65			**$950,255.16**	
Contribute for 20 years				
Contribution Years	20	45	20	Years
Contribution Amount			$ (10,000.00)	
Interest Rate			4.00%	
Total at age 45			**$297,780.79**	
Suspend Payments for 5 years				
Accumulated amount			$297,780.79	
Accumulation			5	Years
Contribution Amount			$ -	
Interest Rate			4.00%	
Total at age 50			**$362,295.86**	
Resume Contributions				
Contribution Years	50	65	15	Years
Contribution amount			$ (10,000)	
Interest rate			4.00%	
Total at age 65			**$852,710.25**	
Cost to Retirement Fund			**$97,544.91**	

One strategy would be to contribute toward your child's education closer to your retirement age. By this time, your funds have time to accumulate, and you have a better idea of your retirement income forecast. You could save thousands of dollars to your retirement account and still contribute toward your child's education.

Although your child may have to take out a college loan, they have 40 years of working life ahead of them to accumulate retirement savings. As a parent you have less than half that time.

15. Working your way through college

Working your way through college is not easy. Tough schedules with a heavy study schedule cuts down on your free time. Using that free time to get a paying job is far better than taking out more loans. Working minimum wage for 10 hours a week could save you $18,000.

For example:

- Working 10 hours a week at minimum wage (say $7.00) gives you $280.00 a month or $13,440 over 4 years.

- If you had to borrow that amount as a student loan you would have an additional $149.21 monthly payment on a ten-year loan repayment plan at 6%. That's almost $18,000 over the 10 year period.

16. You've graduated, now what?

a) Doing what you love

If your job, or prospective career, entails something you love doing, the likelihood is that you will be successful within that occupation. Having a passion, and being able to follow that passion, creates joy and happiness, embracing motivation and achievement.

Unfortunately, we live in a society judged mainly by money and materialism so careers are focused on employment that will bring the most money. Not much thought goes into whether you will want to spend 40 to 60 hours a week doing something that you will come to hate….for the rest of your working life.

Being happy at your work is of paramount importance because you will spend so much time there. Probably more time than you spend with your family. This will reflect on your choice of degree and the amount you will spend to obtain that degree. Find the balance that allows you to enjoy a career with maximum enjoyment for maximum salary, for a minimum educational expense. Not an easy task.

Never underestimate the value of attending a community college for two years before going on to a four-year college program. As you mature you will begin to view the world in a wider light which opens up your mind to fresh opportunities. For more information see Chapter Four: Planning

b) Resumes

You have just a few seconds to grab the attention of the person reading your resume. They may have to read several hundred applications for the same job opening so you have to stand out from the others. Unfortunately, there's too much dependence and hope that the resume will get you a job.

- The purpose of the resume is to get **an interview.**
- 40% of the hiring decision is based on personality.
- Keep your resume short and to the point.
- Use simple English. Don't try and impress by using big words.
- The reader has to quickly understand who you have worked for, what the company does, and your responsibilities and achievements within the company.
- Keep it to one page.
- List current work experience first, and work backwards chronologically from there.

17. Chapter Five: Highlights

- There's something wrong with this picture. The government gets paid, lenders are paid, and the universities are getting paid on ever-increasing education costs, faculties are paid with generous benefit packages, and the student loans are footing the bill. The default rate on student loans has increased, and the financial commitment is causing tremendous financial stress on students and graduates alike.
- The repayment of college education costs is a drag on the future spending power and life goals of graduates. Cars, houses, and household goods are not being purchased with a highly negative effect on the economy as a whole.
- Calculate your chosen professions' likely career earnings, and compare your findings with the cost of your degree. Find the lowest level, mid-level and highest level salaries to expect.
- A poor salary expectation with a high college education cost is a recipe for trouble, as the repayment of your loans will be a huge drain on your resources for many years.
- Future education cost reductions will arrive with technology and the internet. It's already playing an active role with the offering of online degrees.
- Apart from the education for your chosen degree, going to college will allow you to receive a great life experience where you mingle in an academic world on a social basis while living away from home, probably for the first time.
- Don't underestimate the fact that a higher education also provides the ability for you to maximize and create connections, and networking opportunities.
- With a degree, you are more likely to be employed than someone with only a high school diploma. You will also earn more too. Associate's degrees paid 30% more than a high school diploma, and a bachelor's degree pays 75% more.
- Education costs are rising at about 6% annually. Reasons include; higher salaries and benefit payments for faculty members to attract the best. Larger number of students

than positions offered, upgrading of facilities and dorm, cafeteria, and security all incur high costs.

- Those with even less than $500 in a college savings account are three times more likely to enroll in college, and 4.5 times more likely to graduate, than those with no savings or savings account.

- There are two types of 529 Plans. The first is Prepaid Tuition Plan only offered by a limited number of states. You are buying tuition at today's prices, with the state assuming any future tuition cost increases.

- The second type of 529 Plan is more common; a College Savings Plan. This operates as an investment fund offering mutual funds, and subject to market variation. It also offers risk, and account and management fees.

- Contributions are not tax deductible. The 529 Fund grows on a tax-free basis. Distribution of funds is free of federal tax but may be subject to tax in some states.

- Contributions as gifts are limited in 2014 to $14,000 per person, although a lump sum donation of $70,000 with the gift reported over five years is allowed. Can only gift cash.

- Contributions are maxed lifetime at $320,000 with some variation according to state.

- You may find that your account choices are limited, and you may only be able to change the account every 12 months.

- There's an advantage to each beneficiary having his or her own separate 529 Plan fund.

- There are a number of disadvantages attached to the 529 Plan. They include: It counts as a parental asset, no accounting of grants and scholarships, limitations on contribution and investment fund choices. You might be stuck with an educational account that can only be liquidated with a penalty.

- The Coverdell ESA is similar to the 529 Plan, except the contributions are smaller at only $2,000 annually, and there are somewhat harsher distribution rules regarding age and earning limitations.

- Roth IRAs and IRAs are both a source to pay qualified education costs. 401(k)s should rollover to an IRA before educations costs can be deducted without tax or penalty.

- Paying for your child's education has a terrible impact on your retirement savings. Let your children take out college loans and then you may help pay the loans off when you have a clear idea of your own retirement.

- Your children have 40 years of working life left to accumulate their own retirement savings. You have less than half that time.

- It is vital to understand the ratio of your college debt to the income you anticipate earning in your chosen career.

- View your college debt as an investment and calculate a realistic return on that investment by knowing your potential lifetime earnings. As with all investments, keeping expenses (college costs) down increases your return. Generally you will probably see a good return if you balanced your loans with your career earnings.

- Benefits of a higher education are not just academic. You are often away from home for the first time (Hooray) and this allows you deal with your financial life outside of the protection of home.

- There is a great opportunity to network and create contacts for future use.

- You will earn significantly more than someone with a high school diploma.

- College costs are rising faster than the rate of inflation and family income.

- There are a number of ways to save for a college education, but the rules vary by state, and change according to political whim.

- Most college savings plans trumpet the tax savings, but play down the associated fees, lack of flexibility, and the significant penalties if the money is not used for higher education purposes.

- The Roth IRA is a very efficient way to pay for higher education.

- There is a significantly detrimental effect on retirement savings if the money is not set aside for retirement but used for college education instead. It is better to save for retirement and help your children pay their college loans off closer to, or after retirement, when you have a better picture.

- There are four steps to help calculate the cost of your college education:

  Cost of college

  Minus

  Financial aid (scholarship, grants, state grants, Pell Grants)

  Equals

  Net cost of college

- Scholarships are grants that do not have to be repaid.

- Pell Grants are generally for financially needy students who have not earned a bachelor's or professional degree. The amount is limited to $5,730 for the year ending June 2015.

- Many people do not do enough homework when researching assistance in the form of grants. Many people are missing this boat because there are numerous grants available some of which are not taken.

- Perkins Loans are offered to financially needy students. There are annual and total loan limits with a repayment period up to 10 years.

- There are thousands of web pages devoted to college loans, the loan process, and definitions of the types of loans.

- Don't forget the Federal Work-Study Program where you are paid through your school for work on and off campus, with the emphasis on your subject or civic education.

- Most students will probably maximize their government loans and have to take a loan from a private lender.

- Government loans include Stafford or Direct Loans. These are further divided by the different qualifying rules for subsidized and unsubsidized loans.

- Direct Subsidized Loans are for undergraduates and based on student need. Interest will now accumulate to the loan balance during the 6 month grace period

- Direct Unsubsidized Loans are for undergraduates but do not include graduate and professional students. Student need is not a factor in loan qualification.

- Direct Plus Loans are for the parents of dependent students including graduate and professional degree students, but are unsubsidized.

- Direct Consolidation Loans: Allows for Direct loans and commercial loans to be consolidated into one loan.

- If you can't pay your student loans, it is possible to obtain deferment and forbearance. Forgiveness is rare unless you are in a profession that allows you to do so after a period of time.

- Defaulting on any loan has a very detrimental effect on your credit. This can mean wage garnishment, loss of state and federal tax refunds, and being reported to a collection agency. Judgments may also be won in court against you resulting in forfeitures of income and property.

- Graduation sees many people opting for a career for financial reward rather than for a passion for the career.

- Don't underestimate the effect on your happiness when you are working 40 to 60 hours a week in a job you hate. The end result may be depression, anger, and disappointment even if you are financially better off.

- Having a passion for your work will result in improved performance, better pay, and quicker advancement.

- Your resume should be short, to the point, and simple. Forty percent of the hiring decision is based on personality. The purpose of your resume is to obtain an interview.

- Be an active networker. As many as 60% of people are finding their job through networking.

chapter six:
i is for insurance

PROTECT YOURSELF; LIFE DOESN'T ALWAYS GO THE WAY YOU PLAN.

Chapter Six focuses on insurance. Descriptions are provided for informational purposes only. Everyone's financial situation is different, and financial purchases should be tailored to the individual. There are no recommendations to purchase products from any particular company. You are strongly advised to consult with experts and licensed professionals, as well as to seek legal and accounting advice, before making your financial decisions.

1. Why should I buy insurance?

Insurance protects you and your family by compensating you from financial loss caused by an unexpected event.

Imagine the peace of mind and confidence you have in knowing that, should unexpected events cause a financial disaster, you're able to say, "I'm covered." And you really are.

In most instances, the financial loss involves damage or loss to:

- car
- house
- health
- employment income
- life
- lawsuit

The terms, and your compensation terms, are outlined in a contract (policy). Your payment for insurance coverage is called a premium.

You probably know:

- Car and homeowners insurance is mandatory and required by state law and lenders.
- Health insurance is very complex and expensive.

You probably don't know:

- In many cases, your auto and homeowners insurance is insufficient protection against an accident involving serious injury.

- The life & disability insurance coverage provided by employers is mostly insufficient to meet the needs of you and your family.

2. Why don't I fully protect myself against an unexpected event?

"I can't afford it" and "I'll take that risk" are among the top responses. For some there will be no convincing otherwise. This applies especially to the young who feel they are invincible.

Try asking yourself some "What if?" questions:

What would happen to my finances and/or my family if I..........?

- Fell sick and couldn't work for the next 3 years?
- Were at fault in an accident, was sued for $1.5 million, and lost?
- Had a remaining parent become totally dependent on me?
- Died unexpectedly?
- Had a loss in any number of similar situations.

Partners and spouses should be involved in financial and insurance discussions. In nearly every case, the effect of being under or non-insured has its biggest effect on the people around you.

3. Insurance companies and agents

a) Types of insurance companies

- Stock owned: These are publicly traded and include Prudential, Alliance, and Metropolitan Life among others. In these companies, the board of directors' first responsibility is to keep the shareholders happy. Policyholders are, by default, a secondary responsibility of the board.

- Mutually owned: Co-op type companies where the policyholder actually owns a piece of the company. Guardian, Ohio National, New York Life, North Western, Mutual Trust, State Farm, and others. Here, the first responsibility of the company board is to the policyholders.

- Insurance companies, especially mutual companies, have performed well in the recession of the 2000s, unlike many of the other financial institutions.

- Many of the companies have been selling insurance a long time. Some life insurance companies have been around for over 150 years, and there's not much they haven't seen, so their risk calculation tends to be very accurate.

- Guarantees offered by an insurance policy are only as good as the company making the guarantee. Take that into consideration when making a decision.

b) Financial strength

You can find the financial strength of any company through one of the following credit monitoring agencies:

- Fitch Ratings

- Moody's Investor Service
- Standard & Poor's Insurance Ratings Services
- A.M. Best

It should be noted that all four agencies have come under intense scrutiny and criticism for their part in the recession beginning in 2007. This criticism came about because the agencies provided favorable ratings to Lehman Brothers and mortgage-backed securities which eventually failed.[29]

In February 2013, the US government filed a civil suit against Standard & Poor's in a California court, seeking damages of $5 billion for the agency's alleged role in misleading investors during the run-up to the financial crisis.[30]

An insurance company has to be licensed by every state in which it does business. Financial regulation in New York is generally regarded as being stricter than most other states, so insurance companies headquartered there are more highly supervised.

Insurance companies are required by states to keep strong liquid reserves, enough to pay all of their contractual obligations. This requirement is one reason they have done so well in the recent recession. There is a movement to change these requirements because the insurance companies want to obtain a better return on their investments.

c) Insurance costs

Auto, homeowners, and term life insurance products provide a very competitive market where it pays to shop prices. However, cost is determined by the coverage, terms, and conditions which should be balanced so you are fully protected at all times.

- To compare coverage on an equal basis you should match each policy's features and benefits. For example: an umbrella liability insurance policy might not cover an uninsured motorist. Similarly, disability insurance policies will likely differ in their interpretation of the word "disability." Each company describes their liabilities differently, meaning you may be covered with one company and not with another.

- Check for features that might prove costly in years to come, such as a non- guaranteed premium, where the insurance company can increase your premium in the future.

- Focus on how the insurance protects you, your family, and your assets, as well as the cost. The internet provides a wealth of information on insurance companies, their products, and their financial condition, but a face-to-face interview with a well-informed and experienced insurance agent is essential. (See Chapter Four: Planning)

d) Service

In television advertising, the insurance claim is settled on the spot by the sudden appearance of a company officer brandishing a check. However, this is very often not the case, and you find out that you swapped a very cheap premium for poor service when you have a claim.

- Your insurance agent should be your savior when you have a claim.

---

[29] Source: *Christopher Alessi, and Roya Wolverson, "Introduction: the Credit Ratings Controversy, Updated: Feb 11, 2013*
[30] *US District Court, Central District of California, US vs. McGraw-Hill Companies and Standard and Poor's Financial Services, LLP.2-4-2013*

- Companies with sophisticated web pages offer you access to your records but sometimes you need to chat live with someone either online or by telephone. Often you end up in voicemail hell which is frustrating.

- Easy and convenient access helps smooth out a lot of irritation.

- The state insurance commissioner's office will reveal complaint records about insurance companies.

- The Better Business Bureau, friends, and co-workers are another source for recommendations and research.

- With all the users on Twitter, Facebook, Google, Yelp, and other forms of social media, it's hard to hide a poor service record.

e) How are insurance agents compensated?

Insurance agents are compensated in various ways, usually with a share of the first year's premium, and a share of the premium as you renew your insurance annually. Life insurance agents are usually compensated more on the first year's premium, and property and casualty agents generally have a bigger percentage of renewal premiums.

Financial companies, including insurance companies, offer financial incentives for their representatives to sell different kinds of financial products, often their most profitable ones. Compensation agreements differ by company.

Many agents do business with a wide variety of companies. Some, commonly referred to as "captive" agents, conduct nearly all their business with one insurance company and are often considered employees of that company

- All insurance agents have to be licensed by the state to sell:

  Property and casualty insurance (auto, home, boat, and liability insurance)

  OR

  Life, disability, and health insurance.

Some agents are licensed to sell both.

- Many insurance agents are also licensed to sell securities (stocks, bonds, retirement plans, and other investment vehicles) and often classify themselves as financial planners.

4. What can cause me financial disaster?

You have a number of different areas to consider:
- Loss or damage to auto
- Loss or damage to home and contents
- Liability from accidents, lawsuit
- Unexpected death, you or a family member

- Loss of salary, wages, and income
- Health issues, you and/or family, short and long term
- Lack of wills, trusts and health directives

5. Auto and homeowners insurance

Example:

You're driving down a busy street texting a friend. You hit and injure someone in a crosswalk. There are several people who witnessed you texting and it's clear that you're at fault. You suffer no injury, but the injured person is taken to the emergency room.

Your car suffers $1,000 in damages and you have a $500 damage deductible on your auto policy.

a) The good news

Your car is completely made whole again for the $500 deductible.

b) The bad news

The injured party is not so lucky:

- Spends two weeks in intensive care
- Released from hospital after one month
- Receives physical therapy for another 14 months
- Is unable to work for two years

Imagine the medical bills, the pain and suffering (physical and emotional), lost wages, and the inability to work.

If you were the injured party, for how much would you sue the driver at fault?

Let's assume just the hospital bills amount to $500,000. Your total liability insurance coverage is only $300,000. How is the balance of $200,000 dollars going to be paid?

The insurance company is only on the hook for the liability limit set out in your policy. You, your family and their assets are liable for the rest.

c) The consequences of being uninsured or under-insured

- Goodbye, savings
- Goodbye, retirement savings
- Goodbye, stocks and bonds
- Hello to salary garnishment
- Hello to bankruptcy
- Hello to food stamps

6. Not having enough liability coverage can bankrupt you.

Most auto insurance is purchased based on cost, deductibles, and minimal protection requirements. Many people buying insurance have an incomplete understanding of the protection, or lack of protection, they purchase.

- Reading detailed contracts is boring but necessary. You need to know how, and when, you are covered or not.

- Reflect again on the potential medical expenses of an injury resulting from the previous example. It's very easy to run up $500,000 or more in medical bills, especially where there are multiple victims.

- Even under the guidance of an agent, most people continue to have inappropriate levels of insurance coverage to cover potential losses because they focus on the premium cost.

- Lost in the rush for smaller insurance premium payments are the real consequences of being under insured.

7. Deductibles: Getting more bang for your buck

Deductibles affect your premium payment. As you shift the risk from the insurance company to yourself by having a higher deductible, your premium decreases. The reverse is also true: a lower deductible will cause a higher premium.

Example:
You're driving down the road and you rear-end another motorist. There are no injuries and you take full responsibility. You and the other driver agree that the damages are $1,000. Your auto insurance deductible is $500.

Do you:

(a) Make a claim and have the insurance company pay?

OR

(b) Pay for the damage out of pocket?

In this case you will almost certainly pay out of pocket which raises a question. If you are prepared to pay $1,000 out of pocket why wouldn't you save some premium and raise your deductible to $1,000?

- Ask your property and casualty agent about the advisability of increasing your deductible within your own comfort level. This will probably save you some premium costs.

- Using one company for your auto, home, and umbrella liability insurance should also give you discounts on premium.

- Make sure the lower premium doesn't mean poor service with endless voicemail and claim settlement delays.

- If the higher deductible works for you and you save some premium, it should be either placed into savings, or used to increase the protection of you, your family, and its assets. Either way, this is not spending money.

8. Umbrella liability policies

Most auto and home policies will have maximum liability coverage. An umbrella policy sits like an opened umbrella, on top of and sheltering your auto and homeowners insurance, providing additional coverage.

- The insurance company usually requires minimum levels of liability coverage on your normal auto and homeowner's policies before they'll approve an umbrella policy.

- For about $300 premium annually per $1 million of coverage, you can cover a lot of liability inexpensively.

- It's one of the most overlooked types of protection.

9. Being financially prepared when you're sick and can't work

Many of you insure your homes, watercraft, autos, and motorcycles but won't insure your biggest asset; your income. It should be called "I can't work because I'm too sick or injured insurance" but its labeled disability insurance which causes prejudice against its purchase.

a) Disability insurance differs from long-term care insurance

Both long and short term disability insurance are designed to *replace income lost* through sickness or accident. Long-term care concerns the **cost of care** when you are disabled for extended periods of time.

Most people offer the following reasons for not having income protection:

- I'm not worried, it probably won't happen to me.

- My employer provides group insurance.

- It's too expensive.

Individual disability insurance is discriminatory. It may not be available to you because of age, occupation, income, or poor health.

Events that cause you to be too sick or injured to work, generally strike like a bolt out of the blue and are life-changing events. The effect on family members can be just as significant because they often end up as caregivers.

Disability does not necessarily mean being confined to a wheelchair. It's the weeks and months of aching pain, nights without sleep, rehab, chemotherapy, and treatment during recovery from sickness more often than injury. Put money worries in that mix and you have a recipe for disaster.

b) "It won't happen to me!"

Approximately 90% of all disability claims are caused by <u>illness</u> not, as most people believe, accident.
The most common cause of new disability claims in 2012[31]

Over 28% were for musculoskeletal/connective tissue disorders which include:

- Neck and back pain
- Joint, muscle, and tendon disorders
- Foot, ankle, and hand disorders

These disorders are often, the result of repetitive stress injuries caused by using a computer, stretching too far and putting your back out, twisting a knee or ankle, and damaging ligaments.

Others claims include:

- Cancer   14.6%
- Injuries/poisoning   10.6%
- Mental/psychiatric   8.9%
- Cardiovascular   8.2%

More than 19.5 million disabled Americans are in their working years of ages 18 to 64.

- The average disability claim lasts just over 2.63 years.[32]
- Just over 1 in 4 of today's 20-year-olds will become disabled before they retire.[33]

Imagine for a moment that you are sick or injured and unable to work for a long period of time, perhaps several years or more:

- Will your spouse/partner's income be sufficient?
- How long will your savings last?
- What lifestyle changes will you have to make?
- What about your future dreams: college for your children, travel, retirement, legacies?
- What would happen to your credit rating and borrowing power?

c) Is Social Security the answer?

A plan dependent on obtaining government support is a losing strategy.

- The average monthly disability benefit is $1,256 for men and $993 for women.[34]
- 70% of claims are denied at the initial level which can take from 3 to 5 months.[35]

---

[31] The Council for Disability Awareness 2013 Long-Term Disability Claims Review
[32] U.S. Census Bureau, American Community Survey, 2011
[33] U.S. Social Security Administration, Fact Sheet February 7, 2013
[34] Source: U.S.Social Security Administration, Office of Retirement and Disability, Fast Facts and Figures about Social Security, 2013.
[35] Source Social Security Disability Fact Sheet & Source: Tim Moore, Social Security Disability Resource Center

- Appeals can take up to 12 months with 80% of appellants still denied.[36]

d) Two choices to help financially with disability

I. Group/Employer-paid insurance

An employer paid plan provides a basic level of benefits, typically 60% of your salary but this is *taxable*.

- High income individuals may receive a much lower percentage of income protection.
- Bonuses and commissions may not be covered at all.
- The benefit is taxable to the extent your employer pays for it.
- Benefit is offset by government programs such as Social Security.
- Coverage can be cancelled or modified.
- Changing employers can cause you to lose protection.

II. Individually-paid insurance policy

When you pay for your own disability policy, you are provided with a basic level of benefits, typically 60% of your salary, but it is *not taxed*. A good insurance company will provide a policy with the following benefits:

- The cost is guaranteed.
- Benefits are not offset by other income sources. It's possible to work in another occupation and still collect a benefit.
- Benefits are tax free.
- Policy benefits cannot be modified.
- Coverage cannot be cancelled.
- Can adjust coverage to meet changing needs.
- Benefits include protection against inflation
- You own the policy. Take it wherever you go.

III. Cost example of an individual disability insurance policy

Your premium will differ by insuring company and according criteria such as your age, health, occupation, and income.

- To obtain a non-taxable benefit of $1,500 monthly, $18,000 annually until aged 65 requires you pay $80 monthly premium on a long term disability policy.[37]
- 30-year-old person.
- Earning $50,000 annually.
- In good health.
- Occupation, sales representative.

---

[36] Source Social Security Disability Fact Sheet & Source: Tim Moore, Social Security Disability Resource Center

[37] *Very approximate, dependent on company and personal circumstances. This was for illustration purposes only.*

Dealing with health problems, emotional and physical recovery, hospital and household bills is not the time to be worrying about losing your income. If you're willing to insure your cars, boats, and motorcycles surely you should insure your biggest asset, your income.

10. Health Insurance/Obamacare

Health insurance is a very complex subject that is in the middle of a massive change. The rollout of the online sites has been the kind of debacle, both financially and effectively, that any government process inevitably causes. It is far too complex to address in detail in this chapter. What follows is very basic outline:

According to the recent Supreme Court decision, the 2012 healthcare law ("The Patient Protection and Affordable Care Act,") also known as Obamacare is a tax.

a) **There are 21 new taxes, some of which are outlined below.**

- A sales tax on health insurance providers which will likely be passed on to consumers.

- For itemized tax returns, tax deductions for medical expenses not covered by insurance will be allowed when more than 10% of adjusted gross income (AGI). This is an increase from the current 7.5%.

- A 0.9% increase in payroll taxes for individuals earning over $200,000, and $250,000 for a joint filers.

- A 3.8% tax on unearned income for individuals earning over $200,000, and $250,000 for joint filers. This includes investments, dividends, annuities, and, royalties. It does not include tax-exempt bonds, veteran's benefits, or qualified plan distributions.

- Capital gain tax on home sales. When the profit is over $250,000 for individuals, or $500,000 for joint filers, it is added to income. The additional difference will be subject to the 3.8% Medicare tax.

- FSA, health savings accounts and medical reimbursement accounts are now restricted to payment for prescription drugs. There is no payment for over-the-counter medication except for insulin.

- FSA accounts are now restricted to a maximum contribution of $2,500 annually. You may use an FSA account for co-pays, deductibles, some drugs, and certain medical equipment.

- No federal subsidy for privately purchased health plans.

- Beginning in 2014, with few exceptions, unless you have government-approved healthcare insurance, you will pay a penalty to the IRS. This penalty is $95 or 1% of income in 2014, rising to $695 or 2.5% of income by 2016.

- Manufacturers of medical devices, wheelchairs, pacemakers, CPAP machines, and other similar equipment will pay a 2.3% sales tax on a taxable medical device. This will likely be passed on to the consumer.

- Employers will pay a 40% excise tax on the portion of a plan where coverage exceeds $10,200 annually for an individual, and $27,500 for a family.

- Companies offering employees medical insurance will pay 2 separate fees:

    i. $1 per employee covered in 2012 and beyond, toward medical research.

    ii. A fee of $63 per employee at the end of 2014 to defray costs of high medical claims.

b) The success of Obamacare depends on the young and healthy

According to the Census Bureau, in 2010 13% of the population were 65 years or older. This will increase to 19% by 2030 and means that the demands on the healthcare system will continue to grow for the next 17 years.

As with any type of insurance, the plan can only work when the majority of policyholders support the claims made by a small minority. For Obamacare to work, the young and healthy, those in their 20s and 30s, will have to sign up in big numbers. They appear unwilling to do so for the following reasons:

- The young tend to think they don't need health insurance. There's a certain air of invincibility that comes with being young.

- The cost of the plans offered would appear to be too expensive and discourage youth from wanting to spend money on something they perceive as unnecessary.

- The penalties appear far too lenient to be effective. Failure to have health insurance will cause a penalty which will be $95 or 1% of income starting in 2014, rising to $695 or 2.5% of income by 2016. Even $695 annually, the penalty in 2016, is less than sixty dollars monthly and far less than the cost of insurance.

c) State healthcare exchanges

These are online sites which will allow you to compare and purchase different health plans which differ widely according to the state and county in which you reside.

Only by purchasing a plan offered through the state exchange can a federal subsidy be obtained, and this also applies to employees where an employer is not offering a health plan. It is complicated, with some states opting out of the federal subsidy program which is administered through Medicaid.

There will be four levels of plans ranging from bronze to platinum, each of which will provide lower co-pays and deductibles for more premiums.

d) Federal subsidies

There will be huge expansion of Medicaid to allow subsidies to defray cost to the participants who purchase plans through exchanges. Healthy people will pay more for their coverage than unhealthy people as the Obamacare model is based on a "community" of people with little regard to individual health experience.

Subsidies are linked to the federal poverty level. The 2013 federal poverty level for an individual is $15,282 up to $94,200 for a family of four. As family size increases so does the federal poverty limit. The 2014 levels show an approximate 1.5% increase in the numbers shown.

Federal Poverty Level Percentages and Family Size[38]

Household Size	100%	133%	150%	200%	300%	400%
1	$ 11,490	$15,282	$17,235	$ 22,980	$34,470	$ 45,960
2	$ 15,510	$20,268	$23,265	$ 31,020	$46,530	$ 62,040
3	$ 19,530	$25,975	$29,295	$ 39,060	$58,590	$ 78,120
4	$ 23,550	$31,322	$35,325	$ 47,100	$70,650	$ 94,200
5	$ 27,570	$36,668	$41,355	$ 55,140	$82,710	$ 110,280
6	$ 31,590	$42,015	$47,385	$ 63,180	$94,770	$ 126,360
For each additional person add	$ 4,020	$ 5,347	$ 6,030	$ 8,040	$12,060	$ 16,080

Your expected contributions are expected to be as follows:

- **Up to 133% of FPL**   **2% of your income**

- **133%-150% of FPL**   **3% - 4% of your income**

- **150%-200% of FPL**   **4% - 6.3% of your income**

- **200%-250% of FPL**   **6.3% - 8.05% of your income**

- **250%-300% of FPL**   **8.05% - 9.5% of your income**

- **300%-400% of FPL**   **9.5% of your income**

e) More items for you to note

- Health insurance companies are required to spend between 80 and 85% of the premium payments received depending on whether it is an individual, small, or large group plan.

- There will be no pre-existing conditions for children. Family policies include children up to 26 years of age.

- Caps and limitation on coverage and exclusions for pre-existing conditions in adults will be prohibited.

- There is a disincentive to work because should you cross the federal poverty level by one dollar in income, you lose your subsidy.

- Married couples will fare worse. They file their income jointly, meaning they will qualify for less of a subsidy than two individuals living together and filing separately.

- Many employers are cutting the hours of employees to less than 30 hours. This enables them to avoid providing a health benefit plan.

- The federal government has already abandoned the mandatory rules applying to employers until 2015.

- By all accounts, from both Republicans and Democrats, the proposed Obamacare is poorly organized, confusing, and in disarray, yet was supposed to have been in place by January 1, 2014. Certainly the roll out of the online registration has been a fiasco.

---

[38] Maggie Mahar, Health Beat Blog, June 27, 2013 and, July 25, 2013,

These are very brief details of a very complex, ever-changing, and politically charged plan. Many more people will be allowed to enjoy medical treatment, but it's going to be much more costly with far less choices than most anticipate.

11. Using tax-free plans and wellness programs to save health costs

Health insurance is very important because the consequence of being under or non-insured is a leading cause of bankruptcy. Some of the rules have changed under Obamacare.

Wherever possible and practicable, you should take advantage of tax-advantaged plans to pay some, or all, of your medical expenses.

Each of the following accounts is a tax-advantaged account, meaning you can deduct qualified medical expenses from your taxes. The terms and conditions vary widely, and you should consult either with your human resource contact, or accountant, to discuss the best plan for your circumstances.

IRS publication 969 gives a thorough outline of each plan. What follows is a partial synopsis:

a) Flexible Spending Account (FSA)

This is arguably the most common tax-free program for health cost savings. You contribute to a flexible spending account with deductions made by your employer from your paycheck before taxes are taken. The funds remain untaxed unless you spend the money on something other than medical expenses.

Among the allowable expenses:

- Health plan co-pays
- Doctor's fees
- Eye exams, eyeglasses, and contacts
- Laboratory fees
- Dental
- Hearing aids
- Prescriptions

You are not allowed to use your FSA for health insurance premiums, Long-term care costs, or amounts covered by another health plan.

- You are allowed to contribute a maximum of $2,500 to your individual FSA plan for 2014, thereafter the contribution will increase based on the rate of inflation
- The "use it or lose it" rules provision has changed. You may now rollover no more than $500 of unused money to the following year.

b) High-Deductible Health Plan (HDHP).

A high-deductible health plan is required before qualifying for some medical plans. It offers the advantages of tax deductions for qualified medical expenses.

HDHPs are defined as an insured or self-insured health plan with a minimum annual deductible. The popularity of this program has increased significantly over the past few yearsv.

This plan is best for the young, healthy, and fit. Not for those with deteriorating health or with pending surgeries.

- In 2014 annual out-of-pocket costs cannot exceed $6,350 for self-only coverage and $12,700 for family coverage.

- In 2014 the annual deductible must be at last $3,300 for single coverage and $6,550 for family coverage.[39]

- Deductibles, co-payments, and other amounts can be included toward your maximum out-of-pocket expenses.

- Contributions made by an employer may not be subject to tax.

c) Health Savings Account (HSA)

You have to be enrolled in a high-deductible health plan (HDHP) to qualify. HSAs are plans for depositing pre-tax money into an account, controlled through an employer or a trustee such as a bank, to pay or reimburse qualified medical expenses.

- Distributions are tax deductible when used for qualified medical expenses even if you do not itemize deductions.

- Contributions remain in the account until used. Earning and interest are tax free.

- An HSA is portable and can be taken with you on change of employment.

d) Medical Savings Accounts (MSA)

You have to be enrolled in a high-deductible health plan (HDHP) to qualify. MSAs were created to help self-employed individuals, and employees of small businesses, meet the cost of medical care. Contributions are made on your behalf to a trust, which then administers the cash balance as payments for qualified medical expenses.

- Distributions are tax deductible when used for qualified medical expenses even if you do not itemize deductions.

- MSAs are portable and can be taken with you on change of employment.

- Contributions remain in the account until used. Earning and interest are tax free.

e) Health Reimbursement Accounts (HRA)

A health reimbursement arrangement (HRA) must be funded solely by an employer. You are not required to be enrolled in a high-deductible health plan (HDHP).

- There are questions concerning the HRA being allowed under Obamacare rules when they are not part of a group health plan.

f) Wellness programs

A survey of nearly 2,000 US employers (representing over 20 million US employees and their dependents) found the following:[40]

---

[39] *Source: Internal Revenue Service, Bulletin 2013-21,* Rev.Proc.2013-25 *5-20-2013 &* Rev.Proc. 2012-26
[40] *Source: Aon Hewitt, the HR consultancy's 2012 Health Care Survey, John Zern & Jim Winkler*

Among those employers using a monetary incentive to promote participation in a program:

- 59% offered for participation in wellness and health improvement programs, up from 37% in 2011.

- 54% offered for participation in disease/condition management programs, almost triple the 17% that did so in 2011.

- 66% offered a health risk assessment, almost double that of 2010.
- 60% offered biometric screening, blood pressure, and body mass index.

12. Life Insurance

Life insurance, like many products in the financial arena, has morphed from a simple choice of two main products, term and whole life or permanent, to three with the introduction of universal life insurance. The first two products have effectively remained the same, but the introduction of universal life spawned a number of different variations and added complexity.

Some life insurance companies have been around as long as 150 years and have continued to pay benefits throughout that period of time. That includes the Great Depression of the 1930s, two World Wars, The Korean War, The Vietnam War, and periods of oil embargos, high interest rates, high inflation rates, huge stock market fluctuations, real estate depression, and the more recent recession of the 2000s.

- Life insurance is only issued with medical underwriting. Some health issues may mean you are uninsurable or insurable only by paying a high premium.

- There is a maximum amount of life insurance that insurance companies will issue to you. Those receiving the death benefit (beneficiary) must have an "insurable interest" meaning that your death will cause them financial loss.

a) Why should I buy life insurance?

Life insurance generally offers you advantages and protection against loss in the following areas:

- Protection for your family by allowing them to maintain the same standard of living.
- Pay outstanding debt
- Pay taxes
- Pay estate taxes
- Business and partner protection
- Fund a business buy-out
- Funding charitable gifts
- Pay estate legal and administrative costs

Whole life or permanent insurance also offers other advantages considered later in this chapter.

b) When do I need life insurance?

Statistics show the normal life expectancy for a male at birth is 75 years, with women living a few years more to 80.[41] People are living longer and healthier. Most of you will die and need the insurance death benefit much later in life, in your 70s, 80s, 90s, and even 100 plus. Purchasing life insurance during those years becomes cost prohibitive owing to age and health.

- Buy life insurance when you're young; premiums are at their lowest and your health is likely at its best.
- You can, if you choose, make sure life insurance is in force whether you die young or very old. (See below: making term insurance a winner).

c) How much life insurance should I buy?

The most appropriate approach to the amount of life insurance you should purchase is defined as the "Human Life or Human Economic Value." In 1927, the book *The Economics of Life Insurance* by Solomon Hebner, outlined the replacement value of human life in economic terms. These principles were broadly adopted when calculating the compensation to the victims of the 9-11 disaster.

Assuming a gross income of $50,000:

- $1,250,000 at an interest rate of 4% would produce $50,000 annually.

- Your dependents would pay taxes on the income generated at ordinary income levels.

- Your individual circumstances will dictate the face amount of the policy. When calculating your income from a face amount, you should use a conservative interest rate. A safe rate not attached to high risk; for example, the stock market.

- The death benefit is generally tax free to the beneficiary (the person named to receive the proceeds from the policy) although a substantial estate could be subject to estate taxation.

- Many people subscribe to a multiple of earnings as a way of calculating the death benefit. For example, 30 times earnings for a younger person's coverage, or 20 times earnings for someone in their 40s. Using actual earnings with some projections for potential salary increase and inflation creates a more accurate figure.

d) How do I know which type of insurance is best for me?

Different people have different needs. You should choose a life insurance product that will suit those needs. At the same time, if you can afford the premium, whole life insurance offers significant advantages and guarantees over all the other policy types.

Policies other than whole life shift the risk of loss from the insurance companies to the insured, and in return offer a cheaper premium, the chance of better investment results on the cash value, and/or the ability to adjust the death benefit as the insured requires.

The strongest position is to have as much whole life as you can afford backed up with a term policy which can be converted to a strong whole life policy at a time that suits your income. The total amount of insurance coverage should equal your economic value.

---

[41] *Source: The Census Bureau, table 104 Expectation of Life at Birth, 1970 to 2008, and Projections, 2010 to 2020*

13. Term life insurance

Term insurance is like car insurance; it pays as long as the policy is in force. There are two main types, annual renewable term and level term. Neither has a cash value.

- Term insurance is good for the young and the financially challenged, and is better than nothing.
- It's inexpensive compared to other types of insurance because there is no investment creating cash value. Also the risk of you dying while it's in force is small.
- Most advertisements for life insurance are targeting inexpensive premiums, which means term insurance.
- Some polices will allow for a return of premium if the death benefit is not paid out during the term of the policy. There is an additional cost whether this is a rider, or part of the policy. You have to calculate whether these extra costs offer an overall benefit to you.
- Statistics overwhelmingly show that term insurance is not in place at the time of the insured's death. The insurance company avoids suffering its biggest loss, paying your death benefit. In effect you will have lost all the term premiums you've paid, the death benefit, and the opportunities to invest either.

a) Annual renewable term:

This term insurance policy renews each year without the need for medical underwriting so, in effect, it could be purchased each year until you die. It certainly offers the most inexpensive form of insurance **but:**

- The increasing term premium expense usually becomes economically impossible at some point, usually around retirement age, and the insured allows coverage to lapse.

b) Level term

Your life insurance policy has fixed premium payments with a fixed death benefit for a pre-determined period of time, for example 10, 20, or 30 years.

- Your policy is in force as long as you make the premium payments during the time period selected. The insurance then expires.

- Upon expiration of your policy, you will be unable to renew or obtain a replacement without undergoing medical underwriting.

- As you age, you're more at risk for health issues and can become uninsurable or only insurable for a much higher premium.

c) Making your term life insurance a long-term winner

As your assets increase and your life changes, permanent insurance will probably become desirable.

- Make sure the term policy you buy has an endorsement allowing you a conversion to a permanent /whole life policy without any further medical underwriting.

- There will be a small charge to have the conversion clause in the term policy, but it is well worth it.

- No two companies are the same and neither are their insurance policies. If you want to be able to convert your term policy and make it permanent, then you must be sure that the permanent policy offered is a sound investment. Generally, inexpensive term products do not offer a conversion to the better whole life products.

14. Permanent/Whole life insurance

Whole life policies are an investment with guarantee on the premiums, cash value, and death benefit. They are designed so the cash value equals the death benefit at a specified age, this is known as endowment.

The cash value grows in the same way as a Roth IRA, tax free growth and tax free on withdrawal. Permanent/whole life insurance has better overall benefits than a Roth by offering high limit contributions, performance guarantees, and a death benefit. It is more expensive than term insurance because it is an investment.

Whole life insurance premiums are guaranteed and designed to be sufficient to pay:

- The death benefit
- Policy expenses
- Company profits
- Surrender benefits

Other features of a whole life policy include:

- A guaranteed level premium for the life of the policy. This means that you are paying a higher premium in the early years for the death benefit as compared to a term policy. These "overpayments" and earnings compound tax free, create cash value, and reduce company risk.

- Companies also pay a non-guaranteed dividend based on company performance. (See below: Dividends).

- A cash value account allowing the availability of liquid cash to the policy owner.

- A guaranteed death benefit paid to your beneficiary when you die.

- Strong guarantees on performance

- No tax on growth.

- No tax on death benefit (except possible estate tax).

- Some of your premium purchases more insurance, and some of it adds to the guaranteed cash value.

- Generally, you will earn about 4% (after tax) on your cash value over the life of the policy.

- Accessing your cash value is done through a loan from the insurance company secured by your accumulated cash value.

- When you access your cash value, the death benefit is reduced by a similar amount.

- Insurance companies charge interest on the loan, which is secured by the cash value. You should treat this loan as any other and pay it back.

- You don't have to qualify for the loan from your cash value, and your repayment options are set on your own terms.

- Your goal is to restore the policy to its original state. You should at least pay the annual interest on the borrowed money, otherwise the policy protection can be damaged

- The policy remains in force until your death, unless you stop paying the premiums. The insurance company cannot cancel or alter your policy.

- You can obtain default (lapse) protection if you're sick or injured.

- Many policies contain a provision allowing you to obtain an advance of a portion of the death benefit if you are suffering from an illness likely to lead to death within 12 months.

- Most states allow protection from creditors for life insurance proceeds.

- Life insurance death benefits pass tax free to the beneficiary, with the possible exception of estate taxes.

15. Dividends

Life insurance companies pay dividends when investment performance has been better than anticipated, expenses are lower than anticipated, and fewer than anticipated claims have been paid.

In a stock company, dividends paid benefit the stockholders whether they hold individual life insurance policies or not.

With a mutual company, with participating policies, the dividends are given to the policyholders in the form of "return of excessive premium." They are therefore tax free. Unlike the cash value and death benefit, dividends are not guaranteed. The dividend history of most insurance companies is usually available upon request.

Once the dividend has been paid, the value increases in cash, and death benefit can never be withdrawn.

Dividends can be used in a number of different ways:

- Taken in cash

- Applied to reduce premiums

- Accumulate with interest

- Purchase additional insurance

- Repay loans borrowed from cash reserves

16. Four more advantages of owning whole/permanent life insurance

When asked, most people want to create more wealth with the ability to spend and enjoy that wealth. Many people create wealth but have no ability to spend and enjoy it during their lifetime because they fear running out of money. They live on the interest created by the principle. Whole life insurance offers a great solution to this problem.

Whole/permanent life insurance should be a central part of your financial planning. It can be used in numerous advantageous ways in your financial life.

Retirement planning: You can generate significant additional income during retirement by spending down assets you've worked hard to build knowing that life insurance will refill the coffers.

College education: A great savings tool backed up by a death benefit at low cost. Planned correctly, this will last a child their entire lifetime, including paying for their college education. The cash value does not count as an asset for college loan purposes.

Estate planning: Generally regarded as the best financial ally when death occurs.

Reverse mortgage: The life insurance can repay a reverse mortgage after the death of the house owner saving the home for the heirs.

Business planning: Life insurance is used in many aspects of business, protection from owner death, partner death, deferred compensation, and more.

17. Buy term and invest the difference

Many people, including some financial advisors, say that whole life insurance is a poor investment being too costly and you can do better by investing elsewhere. They advise the purchase of a less expensive term policy. The difference between the cost of a premium for a whole life policy, and the less expensive premium for the term policy, is invested into a vehicle giving a greater return, for example the stock market.

- Most people lack the discipline needed to reinvest the difference between the term and whole life premium consistently over 20 or 30 years.

- Such advisors usually quote the cost of insurance and insurance company profits as items the investors will also save. Ignored are the loads and carrying costs of the other investments.

- Totally ignored are the lost opportunity costs on both the premium and the lost death benefit on the term policy when the policy expires or lapses.

- Obtaining a higher rate of return without much higher risk is difficult when, from a cash value standpoint, the **after-tax return** over the life of the policy is guaranteed at about 4%. That's comparable to over 7% before federal taxes, and more if you include state taxes.

- There is no accounting of the risk of the other investment losing value, maybe all of its value. You're taking on substantially more risk to chase the potential of higher rate of return.

- Under this strategy, buying term insurance means you will have probably have no life insurance at death. With whole life, the death benefit will be there when you need it; likely in your mid-70s through 100 plus.

- The real argument is about the ability to have inexpensive insurance while you become self-insured by building up a larger nest egg. The vast majority of people have no hope of building a nest egg matching an insurance policy death benefit.

- **Maybe these advisors should wonder why most, if not all, small and large financial institutions have invested heavily in whole life products, for example:**

a) To offset their employee benefit costs

b) To enhance the balance sheet and diversify their portfolios

It's clear that such financial institutions recognize that whole life insurance is one of the best investments you can make.

18. Universal life insurance (UL)

These policies are more expensive than a term policy, but less expensive than a whole life policy and still have a cash value account. Mainly for people who want to have the flexibility to vary the amount of premium, the interest on the cash value and/or be able to adjust the death benefit during the term of the policy as their circumstances change. This type of insurance is a term policy accompanied by a cash value account.

The simplest way to think of a UL policy is to compare it to leaky bucket. Your premium goes into the bucket and builds up a cash value depending on the type of UL purchased. The bucket (cash value) has some leaks:

- One leak out of the bucket is the annual mortality and expense charges.

- Another leak is the term premium amount.

- The remaining amount in the bucket accumulates according to the UL purchased.

- As you age, the term insurance becomes more costly, and the leak in the bucket gets bigger. Mortality and expense charges are not guaranteed and can also increase.

- Increases in costs can cause the policy to lapse unless there is an increase in premium payments to cover the shortfall.

- Guarantees are not as strong as with a whole life policy, but there are some guarantee clauses you can purchase to prevent a lapse in protection.

- Beware of insurance illustrations which are too optimistic on interest rate expectation.

- Borrowing against your cash value in a universal life insurance policy is generally inadvisable. However, as long as there is enough money in the cash value bucket to pay the premium, the policy will continue to offer coverage.

The different types of UL policies and their characteristics:

a) **Universal life insurance without secondary death benefit guarantees**

- Low premium with plenty of flexibility
- An adjustable death benefit
- The insurance company can increase all expenses
- Almost no guarantees
- Policyholder has a risk of paying a higher than anticipated premium to keep the policy from lapsing

a) **Universal life insurance with secondary death benefit guarantees**

- Guaranteed low premium
- Premium remains flexible but changes can cause lost guarantees
- High expense loads
- No potential for better than guaranteed results
- Little ability to adapt the policy to change

c) **Variable universal life insurance (VUL) (without guarantees)**

Insurance agents have to be licensed to sell securities before they can sell VUL policies. These are similar to UL policies except the cash value return is typically allocated to sub-accounts linked to stock and money market accounts.

- The policyholder controls the investments creating the cash value.
- The policyholder faces higher premium if the investment returns are insufficient to maintain the policy.
- The sub-accounts can be extremely volatile which can adversely affect the performance of the policy.

d) **Variable universal life insurance (with guaranteed death benefit)**

- A hybrid of a VUL and a UL having a secondary death benefit guarantee
- High charges for the guarantees
- Higher guaranteed premium than with a UL

e) **Equity-indexed universal life (EIUL)**

- The policy's cash performance is linked to an index, for instance, the S&P 500.
- Usually very high expense loads
- Similar to a UL with certain guarantees on the cash value
- Offers flexibility on timing and amount of premium payments

Always be aware that with any EIUL or VUL policy you have a substantial risk losing not only the cash value but also any life insurance coverage. Good luck!

19. Group life insurance

Most people rely on the life insurance provided by their company as a benefit. It's usually calculated as a multiple of your annual salary, for example 4 times annual salary. You may well be making a contribution toward the premium through a payroll deduction as well.

- The life insurance provided is almost certainly term insurance.
- Death Benefit greater than $50,000 death benefit it can be taxable.
- The policy is not always portable when you change employment.

Using a multiple of your salary is ill advised. Calculate the amount of insurance needed to replace income. Purchase your own individual policy, and obtain the correct coverage together with the flexibility it offers.

20. Second to die or survivor life insurance

This is a very common estate planning strategy to cope with expected estate taxes. Estate taxes are due and payable at the time of the death of the second spouse. This type of insurance pays a death benefit on the death of the second spouse. The lack of a death benefit on the death of the first spouse is a major flaw because:

- The surviving spouse has to continue premium payments until their own death.
- The surviving spouse loses the opportunity to invest the first spouse's death benefit.
- This can be a multi-million dollar mistake when the first spouse has a premature death and the survivor lives a long life.
- It is much cheaper than permanent/whole life insurance which makes it attractive to an insured who is not fully informed of the potential losses.

21. What is Long-term care (LTC)?

Long-term care concerns the **cost of care** when you are disabled for extended periods of time. For example: paying for the cost of a stay in a nursing home. Long-term care is not professional medical care; it's planning for the long term and removing some of the financial and emotional risks attached to being unable to adequately care for yourself.

You probably know someone who is caring for an ailing grandmother, grandfather, mother, father, sister, or brother. It's not just the aged either. Forty percent of people needing long-term care are between the ages of 18 and 64.

- To qualify as needing long-term care, you will be unable to perform normal everyday tasks known as "activities of daily living" (ADLs). They include dressing, washing, eating, grooming, and other routine daily activities.

- Nursing home care now costs nearly $100,000 annually and in-home help is about $25 an hour. These costs vary by region but remain extremely expensive.

- Most people are incapable of paying a minimum additional monthly payment for basic care.

- Government programs, the Veteran's Administration, Medicare, and Medicaid are not designed to pay for long-term care and provide very limited benefits for limited periods of time.

Failure to develop a plan for care will likely create two sets of consequences to the detriment of:

1. The emotional and physical well-being of your caregivers, who are normally family members, especially the females in the family.

2. Your retirement account, which wasn't intended to pay for your care.

   a) Long-term care insurance

The experience of insurance companies with long-term care insurance is limited as it's a comparatively new product. Premiums on the insurance saw some sharp raises as the policies began to sell on an increasing scale but as the insurance companies realized the true risk of long term care they began to focus on tightening criteria including medical conditions. Some insurance companies stopped selling LTC insurance. The result is that dramatic unexpected premium increases are rarer and premium increases have leveled off in the last 10 years or so. However, until the insurance companies can truly calculate their risk and reward, premium are likely to increase. LTC insurance is still a better deal than paying for Long Term Care facilities out of pocket.

It should be noted that Obamacare took the LTC provision out of the plan as being unworkable.

Otherwise long-term care insurance provides

- Income to pay for the types of care your family should not have as a burden.

- Income to allow your spouse to be a spouse and not a full time caretaker.

- Allows your children to maintain their relationship with you as children, not providing care.

- It is not designed to protect assets.

- It is designed to protect your retirement accounts which are there to support your lifestyle and the prior commitments to your family.

- The premiums on qualified long-term care policies (those with certain defined benefits) are tax deductible. For example, the deductible premium for a person aged between 60 and 70 is $3,640 annually. It should be noted that the deductibility is now limited to medical expenses in excess of 10% of adjusted gross income. Those aged 65 in 2013 though 2016 will be allowed the 7.5% rate.

- Note that federal employees, under a program sponsored by the Office for Personnel Management, and eligible for the Federal Employees Benefits Program (FEHB), qualify for the Federal Long-Term Care Insurance Program.

b) State partnership programs

Most people will require some form of long-term care during their lifetime. They will have to deplete their assets before they can qualify for Medicaid to pay for their care.

The partnership program is collaboration between states and private insurers on the issue of long-term care insurance products. Purchasers of the product can protect some of their assets because the Medicaid limit on the value of assets they may keep is raised.

There is some doubt as to the success of this program among its target audience, the middle class.[42]

c) Life insurance and long-term care

Some companies have introduced a hybrid policy combining the ability to fund long-term care along with a death benefit. In the event that the policy is not used for long-term care then the policy pays a benefit on death of the insured.

- These policies are often funded with a single premium.

- Funding of care costs is usually limited to between 2 and 5% of the death benefit.

Before making a decision on what's best for your individual long-term care needs, it's essential that you meet with a qualified and licensed long- term care professional.

22. Annuities

An annuity is a tax-deferred investment vehicle designed to provide an income stream during retirement.

- It accumulates on a tax free basis but you are taxed on ordinary income levels on the growth when you start to receive the income stream.

- If you take payments prior to age 59.5 years you may also be subject to additional penalties.

The annuities can be of the following type:

a) Fixed

Your money grows at an interest rate determined by the insurance company.

- Payments can be made for a definite period: 10, 15, 20 or other amount of pre-determined years. Should you die in the meantime, the benefit will stop, and there are no provisions for heirs.

- The insurance company will pay out any remaining amount you paid into the annuity as a death benefit.

- Payments can also be made for an indefinite period: your lifetime or the lifetime of you and your spouse if you've taken a survivorship option.

---

[42]   Source: *The Impact of the Partnership Long-term Care Insurance Program on Private Coverage and Medicaid Expenditures Haizhen Lin and Jeffrey Prince, February, 2013*

b) Immediate

This annuity is usually bought with a lump sum with guaranteed payments and interest starting almost immediately. The term of the payments can be for your life or a specified period of time, 10 or 20 years for example.

c) Indexed

The return on the annuity is linked to an index, such as the S&P 500 with some values guaranteed, regardless of the index performance.

d) Variable

You choose from a variety of funds and the performance of those funds dictates the return you will get. Unless you choose a definite period, the payments are based on the amount the annuity has grown and your life expectancy.

e) Fees

Fees on an annuity purchase can be surprisingly high.

- Surrender charge: It is likely you will incur severe penalties for early withdrawal of your money especially during the first 5 to 7 years of the term.

- High annual fees: Variable and indexed annuities can have comparatively high fees. Be cautious and know the fees and expenses before purchase.

23. Chapter Six: Highlights

- Insurance protects you against financial loss from an unexpected event. Imagine the peace of mind and confidence you have when, in the face of a financial disaster, you can say, "I'm covered."

- In most cases you are protecting yourself against financial loss from damage or loss of a car, house, health, employment income, life, or lawsuit.

- Most people avoid insuring themselves with the reasons: "I can't afford it" or "I'll take that risk."

- Always ask the question, "What happens if I/we fell sick and couldn't work for a couple of years, were sued after a car accident for $1.5 million and lost, had a remaining parent become totally dependent on you, or other similar situations?"

- Partners and spouses should be involved in financial and insurance discussions. In most cases, the effect of being under or non-insured has its biggest effect on the people around you.

- Insurance companies are stock or mutually owned. Stock companies are run for the benefit of the stockholders. Mutual companies are run for the benefit of the policyholders.

- Insurance companies are required by statute to keep strong liquid reserves and have generally done well compared to other financial companies in the financial debacle of the 2000s.

- Insurance costs are very competitive but you get what you pay for. Be sure to compare coverage on an equal basis by matching similar policy features and benefits. Focus on what's good for you and your family.

- The financial strength of insurance companies is monitored through A.M. Best Company, Fitch Ratings, Moody's Investors Services and Standard & Poor's Insurance Ratings Services.

- When it comes to service, your insurance agent should be invaluable.

- Insurance agents work on commission sales. They are either brokers doing business with a wide variety of companies, or captive agents who work mainly with a single company.

- All agents are licensed by the states in which they do business. They sell property and casualty insurance, or life, disability, and health insurance. Some agents sell both.

- Insurance agents are often licensed to sell securities. To sell some insurance and annuity products they have to be so licensed.

- Compensation is usually a share of the first year's insurance policy premium, with a continuing smaller share as the policy is renewed.

Auto, home, and liability insurance

- Liability insurance is vital and often underestimated especially when compensation for injury is taken into consideration. The insurance company is on the hook for the liability limit set in the policy. You are liable for the rest.

- Auto insurance is mostly purchased on cost, deductibles, and minimal protection. Again, make sure your liability insurance is appropriate to your situation.

- Umbrella liability policies are an inexpensive way to maximize your liability coverage.

- Insurance premiums are lower when deductible limits are higher. Your deductible should be appropriate to the dollar limit which you are prepared to pay out of pocket before making a claim.

"I can't work because I'm too sick or injured" insurance.

- People seem to be unaware, or not care, that their biggest asset, their income, remains unprotected even when everything else in their life is protected through insurance.

- Income protection is called disability insurance but should be called, "I can't work because I'm too sick or injured" insurance. Ninety-two percent of all claims are for illness, not as most people believe, injury.

- Thirty-five percent of disability claims involve neck and back pain, joint, muscle and tendon disorders, and foot, ankle, and hand disorders.

- Disability does not necessarily mean being confined to a wheelchair. It's the weeks and months of aching pain, nights without sleep, rehab, chemotherapy, and treatment during recovery from sickness more often than injury. Put money worries in that mix and you have a receipt for disaster.

- Social Security is hard to get approved and provides an average monthly benefit of only $1,129.

- Employer-paid disability insurance is taxable. Individual-purchased disability insurance is tax free and provides much more coverage and guarantees than employer-paid policies.

Health insurance

- Health insurance is undergoing tremendous change with the introduction of Obamacare which has introduced 21 new taxes to help fund coverage.

- For Obamacare to succeed, the young and healthy have to sign up in big numbers. They may be unwilling to do so because they don't feel at risk. The coverage is comparatively expensive, and the penalties for not signing on are too small.

- Healthy people will pay more for their healthcare because cost is based on a "community experience" with little regard for an individual's actual health experience.

- People will sign up for Obamacare through state run exchanges where they will qualify for various premium subsidies depending on their income.

- There are no pre-existing conditions preventing insurance being issued. There are no lifetime treatments limits.

- Federal subsidies will be issued depending on either an individual's or a family's income when compared to the Federal Poverty Level.

- Married couples filing jointly may fail to qualify for a subsidy whereas two individuals filing separately would qualify.

- There are a number of programs providing for use of pre-tax dollars to pay for medical costs. These include FSA, HDHP, HAS, MSA, and HRA plans. You are encouraged to use whatever plans are available to you to pay for your health costs with pre-tax dollars.

- Employers are increasingly using wellness programs to encourage good health among their employees.

Life insurance

- The appropriate amount of life insurance to purchase is based on the "Human Life Value" approach, which is based upon replacing the income of the deceased. You would need $1,500,000 in insurance proceeds earning 4% annually to replace a gross income of $60,000 annually.

- Normal life expectancy for both males and females means, for the vast majority, an insurance policy pays off during ages between 75 and 100. Obtaining insurance during these ages is generally cost prohibitive owing to age and health.

- Life insurance is only issued with medical underwriting; you may be uninsurable or only insurable at a high premium.

- There is a maximum amount that insurance companies will issue to an individual and death has to cause financial loss to the beneficiary.

- Term insurance is good for the young and the financially challenged; it's inexpensive compared to other types of insurance because the risk of you dying when it's in force is small.

- Term insurance can be purchased for life, but the premium increases with age. It generally becomes economically difficult after retirement age because the risks of dying are greater, the premium costs are too high, and the odds are that you will drop the policy.

- It's possible to buy term insurance at fixed premium levels for pre-determined periods of time. At the end of the time period, the policy expires and you have to qualify medically to reinsure. You will have aged and may have health problems which could make obtaining insurance more expensive or difficult.

- Statistics overwhelmingly prove that term insurance is not in place at the time the original insured dies. The insurance company avoids paying its biggest expense, the death benefit.

- You make your term insurance a winner by purchasing, for a small charge, the ability to convert term policy to a whole/permanent life policy without having to go through medical underwriting.

- Permanent or whole life insurance is more expensive than term insurance but is classified as an investment as opposed to a cost. Whole life policies offer a cash savings account as well as a death benefit. It has similar tax advantages to a Roth IRA with better performance guarantees, high contribution levels, and a death benefit.

- Generally the return on your cash values is about 4% guaranteed and tax free. This is probably equivalent to a 7% pre-tax rate of return.

- You access the cash value as a loan from the insurance company secured by your cash values. You should always have a plan to pay back the borrowed money to keep the policy intact. Repayment options are entirely up to you.

- Your life insurance can also provide protection against disability and long-term care. Access to the death benefit can be obtained if you are within 12 months of imminent death.

- Whole/Permanent life insurance grows through non-guaranteed dividends. With a mutual insurance company, the policyholder owns part of the company so dividends are tax free and regarded as return of excess premium. Stock company dividends are paid to stockholders.

- Whole/Permanent life insurance should be the central supporting pillar in your financial planning. It helps accelerate and improve retirement, college education, estate, reverse mortgage, business planning, and much more.

- Take the "buy term and invest the difference" theory under advisement because it's not wise planning. Permanent insurance is more expensive than term insurance. The idea is to purchase the term insurance and invest the difference between the payments in a higher earning investment. This strategy is flawed. No account is taken of potential losses in the higher investment, the lost opportunity costs, no guarantees, and the likelihood that no death benefit will be paid at death.

- The argument relies on you building up a sufficient nest egg to become self-insured. Only a minimum of people will realize this objective.

- The argument that whole life insurance is a poor investment is negated by the fact that small and large financial institutions have heavily invested in whole life products to diversify their portfolios as well as offset employee benefit costs.

Universal and variable universal life insurance

- **Universal life insurance** is cheaper than whole/permanent life insurance. It offers a term policy and a cash value. It offers more flexibility in terms of the cash accumulation and death benefit depending on life circumstances.

- Its biggest drawback is the price of the increasing term, mortality, and expense charges which can exceed the interest rate earned on the cash value. This can cause the policy to lapse without adding additional premium.

- You can buy secondary death benefit guarantees, but there is little ability to adapt the policy to change and there's no potential for better than guaranteed results.

- **Variable universal life insurance** is similar to a universal life except the cash value is linked through sub- accounts to stock and money markets. This provides the opportunity to have a high gain in cash value in exchange for the high risk of losing everything.

- It features higher charges to pay for the guarantees with a higher guaranteed premium than a universal life policy.

- **Equity-indexed universal life insurance** features the cash value performance linked to an index such as the S&P 500. Usually it has very high expense loads but does have certain guarantees and flexibility on timing and amount of premium payment.

- With any form of universal life insurance, using your cash value as a source to borrow from is generally ill-advised.

Other life insurance

- **Employer-paid life insurance:** To the extent that an employer pays the life insurance premium, the benefit can be taxable. It cannot generally be taken with you in a job change, and usually provides inadequate protection for you and your family.

- **Estate planning:** Second to die life insurance is often used to pay anticipated estate taxes which are due on the death of the second spouse. It provides little flexibility and can cause financial loss especially when the first spouse has a premature death and the second spouse lives a long time.

- **Business insurance:** Life insurance is used extensively within companies to protect the company against financial loss caused by the death of a partner, employee, or others important to the business.

- **Retirement planning:** Whole life insurance provides the opportunity to maximize retirement income and assist strategies such as reverse mortgage.

- **College planning:** All of the benefits of a Roth IRA as a savings tool, without the handicaps of contribution limits or access to your money. Structured correctly, the cash value will not count as an asset for college aid purposes.

- Whole life insurance should be the central part of your financial planning strategy.

Long-term care insurance

- Long-term care concerns the **cost of care** when you are disabled for extended periods of time. When you need long-term care you will be unable to perform all or some everyday activities of normal daily living. This includes dressing, eating, washing, and grooming.

- Long-term care insurance is designed to provide the type of care your family members should not have to undertake. It allows your spouse and children to avoid being full-time caregivers, and protects your retirement accounts from depletion.

- Long-term care insurance originally experienced substantial increases in premium and lower benefits. The experience of the insurance companies was insufficient to be able to judge long-term care costs against profit. The last 10 years has seen stability in premium increases but insurance companies continue to tighten the conditions to reduce risk.

- States, understanding that LTC is throwing a huge burden on resources, are partnering with long-term care insurance providers to provide products. The concept is that the State will pay for benefits up to the amount contributed by the insured.

- Some life insurance companies have introduced a hybrid policy combining the ability to fund long-term care costs along with a death benefit. These are often funded as a single premium meaning a substantial upfront payment.

- You should meet with a qualified and licensed long-term care specialist to determine what's best for your situation.

Annuities

- An annuity is a contract with an insurance company where you pay either a lump sum or a series of payments to accumulate interest and provide you with an income stream at a predetermined time and amount.

- Annuities can be fixed, immediate, variable, or indexed.

- Fees and penalties can be surprisingly high.

chapter seven:
f is for fitness

LIKE ANY SUCCESSFUL ATHLETE, BUILD
RESERVES TO GIVE YOU STRENGTH.

Chapter Seven focuses on fitness. Descriptions are provided for informational purposes only. Everyone's financial situation is different, and financial purchases should be tailored to the individual. There are no recommendations to purchase products from any particular company. You are strongly advised to consult with experts and licensed professionals, as well as to seek legal and accounting advice, before making your financial decisions.

1. Why do I need a cash reserve?

These reserves are for an emergency, such as when:

- You've lost your job
- Your spouse lost their job
- You've accrued medical expenses
- You contract a long-term illness
- You suffer an injury through an accident
- You experience an unexpected family death
- You have to pay an unfavorable lawsuit settlement
- To cover house or car damage not covered by insurance

2. How much should I have in available cash reserves?

All the financial experts agree that you should have a cash reserve for emergencies. They disagree, however, on the amount. It's a safe bet that if you have three to six months of income in an easily liquidated form for emergencies, that you have a comfortable cushion.

- Saving six months of income as a cash reserve provides a great cushion. If your income is just over $4,100 a month ($50,000 annually) you should be saving just over $400 a month for five years.
- This sounds intimidating, and even disheartening, especially when trying to raise a family on this amount of income.

- It's always best to start small and work your way forward.
- Think in terms of your monthly expenses first. Start setting aside your emergency fund to cover these first of all. When you set aside enough to cover one month's expenses, work on the second month and so on.
- Your first goal might be to set aside $1,000 toward those monthly expenses.

3. **What expenses are covered by my emergency fund?**
    - Mortgage, rent, taxes, and homeowners/renters insurance
    - Debt: Continuing to pay credit cards, autos loans, and other consumer debt
    - Transport: Auto costs, bus fares
    - Health, life, and disability insurances
    - Food and necessary household items

Having an unexpected event can be a devastating both emotionally and financially. This is not the time to be worrying about money for groceries. A cash cushion gives you time to consider your next action in a calm and measured fashion.

a) **Identify waste**

The first area to identify falls in the discretionary spending area. Look at where you can save money, but don't completely have to sacrifice your lifestyle. (See Chapter One: Savings)

- Your budget should include putting money into an emergency fund until you reach a level that equals six months' salary.
- Eating out and buying coffee: Cut this amount in half and put one-half into your emergency fund account.
- Cable TV: Examine your viewing habits and you may find you don't watch all of the channels to which you subscribe. Watch more online and cut the bill.
- Spare change: You will be surprised at the speed you can collect $100 to put toward emergencies.
- Tax refunds: An excellent way to get a head start on your fund.
- Salary Increases: Set aside a portion of your raise as a contribution to the account.

b) **Interest rate expectations**

It is important that you don't get hung up on interest rates for money in your emergency reserves. The fact that your money must be readily available to you means that you will be using accounts with lower interest rates. However, they should be federally guaranteed accounts up to $250,000.

c) **Can my emergency fund be used to invest in opportunities?**

The short answer is no. Your emergency fund is for emergencies and nothing more. Putting your cash at risk for an investment opportunity is not good planning unless you have sufficient liquid reserves saved.

d) Cash reserves versus retirement savings

Cash reserves are for the immediate. Retirement money is for the future, which in some cases is 20 – 30 years away.

The pressure to put money into a retirement program is enormous. It's made easy through your employment as it is taken from your salary before you see it. The fact that it's not subject to tax at that time makes it seem even more attractive. The program is also sold by emphasizing the amount you lose in the long term if you delay making a contribution.

The problem comes when you have an emergency and need ready access to cash. You have a limit on the amount you can take from your retirement fund, and if you don't put it back within this time limit, you're penalized and have to pay taxes on the amount you took out.

As a compromise, you could contribute enough money into the retirement account to meet a company match, and then put additional savings into an emergency fund.

e. Imagine the confidence ….

When you have cash reserves to last at least six months your confidence and optimism will increase dramatically. You know that you've prepared as best you can to deal with a worst-case financial scenario. You are guaranteed to be very happy when you achieve this goal.

4. Book Seven: Highlights

- Experts agree that you should have a cash reserve for emergency purposes, and although they disagree on the amount, having six months of income is a comfortable cushion.

- If you feel six months of income is too tough a target for you, concentrate on getting six months of expense coverage started. Start with a $1,000 and move forward from there.

- You need the cushion in the event of job loss, illness, unexpected accident, damage not covered by insurance, or other unforeseen occurrences.

- Reserves are needed to pay everyday expenses, mortgages, rent, debt payments, commuting to work, health, life and disability insurance premiums, and food.

- You should not expect a high interest rate of return on your emergency reserves. The funds will be placed in safe accounts and readily available so they will not enjoy high interest rates, but they should be protected from loss by the federal government.

- To get started, you should look to cut your discretionary spending. Dining out and cable TV subscriptions probably offer some opportunities to save. Tax refunds and salary increases are other sources.

- It's best to be methodical with saving of small amounts on a regular basis.

- Resist the pressure to put money into a retirement program before building an emergency fund.

- Having cash reserves will cause a great increase in your confidence and happiness.

chapter eight:
y is for you

TAKE ACTION TO ACHIEVE YOUR PURSUIT OF HAPPINESS.

Chapter Eight focuses on you. Descriptions are provided for informational purposes only. Everyone's financial situation is different, and financial purchases should be tailored to the individual. There are no recommendations to purchase products from any particular company. You are strongly advised to consult with experts and licensed professionals, as well as to seek legal and accounting advice, before making your financial decisions.

1. It's in the Declaration of Independence

It's generally agreed that the men who wrote the Declaration of Independence were a wise group of men. Take their advice, and follow the words set out in the second paragraph, where the pursuit of happiness is specifically mentioned.

"We hold these truths to be self-evident, that all men are created equal, that they are endowed by their Creator with certain unalienable Rights, that among these are Life, Liberty and **the pursuit of Happiness."**

Taking action to control your financial life will allow you to follow the advice set down in 1776, and be active in the pursuit of happiness.

These eight chapters, along with the summary ninth, published separately, contain good information on how to conduct your financial life to have the maximum positive impact.

In the end, it will be up to you. Get help where you can. Employ experts, but above all have someone monitor your progress. Nearly everyone needs someone to nudge them when tasks are incomplete or not yet started.

2. Simple reminders to help you take action

Learning what's important is one thing. We generally know whether or not we're in good shape financially, in the same way we know if we're overweight or not. Taking action to correct problems is the biggest challenge because it means change, and making lifestyle changes are very difficult.

- Make a to-do list of tasks which, when accomplished, will make your life happier.
- Have short deadlines.

- Just jump in and get started. Stop procrastinating.

- Make the first task a small task. You will enjoy an easy success quickly.

- Divide big projects into small sub-sets of tasks, wherein completion of each one leads toward completion of the whole.

- Always ask yourself, "What's the next step?"

- Be disciplined and methodical.

- Review frequently.

- Work as a team with your partner/spouse. Motivate each other.

- Reward yourself when you've accomplished a task.

- Plan in an environment that is not distracting. Don't watch TV at the same time you plan.

- Understand the reason for the task in the first place. Concentrate on the positive effect you will realize when it's completed.

- At this point, review Chapter Four: Planning.

3. Doing what you love

If your job, or prospective career, entails something you love doing, the likelihood is that you will be successful within that occupation. You're also very lucky. Having a passion and being able to follow that passion creates joy and happiness, embracing motivation and achievement.

- We live in a society judged mainly by money and materialism, so careers are focused on employment that will bring the most money.

- Not much thought goes the reality of spending 40 to 60 hours a week doing something that you hate….for the rest of your working life.

- Don't underestimate the effect on your happiness when you are working 40 to 60 hours a week in a job you hate. The end result may be depression, anger, and disappointment, even if you are financially better off.

- Having a passion for your work will result in improved performance, better pay, and quicker advancement.

Being happy at your work is of paramount importance because you will spend so much time there. Probably more than you spend with your family. Find the balance that allows you to enjoy a career with maximum enjoyment for maximum salary for a minimum educational expense. Not an easy task.

4. The value of networking

To find your passion try networking. This gives you the maximum chance of making contacts, and through such contacts, finding a valuable connection.

- Networking is very effective for finding new opportunities.

- Friends, previous employers, professional groups and associations, and alumni associations are all places to start making contacts.

- Pick up the phone and call. Don't be shy.

- LinkedIn is a great website for professional contacts.

5.   Being the best you can be

In your life, you will be judged by people outside of your peer group who may have different standards and practices than you. This applies especially at work.

You should be as professional as possible in all aspects of your work. Paying attention to the following points will improve your chances of promotion and salary increases.

- Competence: Clearly, being good at what you do is one of the most important factors in furthering your career.

- Reliability: Others knowing that they can depend on you doing your job to the best of your ability can only enhance your reputation.

- Improving your skills: Taking the time to improve your knowledge, being abreast of the latest developments, and being ahead of the curve counts.

- Communication: Demonstration of good grammar and spelling in reports helps cement your views. There's no distraction for the reader. Performing a spell check before sending an email will show that you care about the way you communicate.

- Punctuality: Habitually being late for meetings shows disrespect to others and yourself. It shows that you are disorganized and unreliable.

- Appearance: Investing in a good wardrobe makes you stand out from others and presents a positive impression.

- Respect: Always show respect to others even if you disagree with their views.

- Politeness: Good manners are always appreciated and, without being obsequious, another way to help you stand out from the crowd.

6.   Consider why you work

- You work for money.

- Money allows a lifestyle.

- Lifestyle allows maximum opportunity for happiness.

Our financial life is generally provided through work. The money we earn makes our lifestyle possible. Make sure your financial house is in order so your lifestyle can provide you with the happiness and joy that will fulfill your life.

Life is about achieving balance. All work and no play makes Jack (Jill) a dull boy (girl). In this way, our lifestyles should be planned to provide us with love, passion, generosity, charity, excitement, enthusiasm, optimism, kindness, bounteousness, anticipation, pleasure, exhilaration, stimulation, animation, and confidence. Get the picture?

- Long hours at work do not translate into efficiency. Plan your workday so you can spend time with your family and loved ones.

- Develop the parts of your life that bring you the greatest joy, such as travel, photography, collecting stamps, running, exercise, canoeing, surfing, paddle boarding, playing with the children, or going on a date with your wife. Or maybe it is just being by yourself.

- Complete yourself by developing the love and joy in your life.

- Start by putting your financial life in order.

Chapter Eight: Highlights

The chapters in this book contain good information on how to conduct your financial life. The real story is that by putting your financial life in order, you will become happier and more confident.

- It's even written in the Declaration of Independence "…..the pursuit of happiness…"

- Taking action is the most difficult part of starting any project, especially when financial in nature. We just don't want to face the truth sometimes.

- Get help. Have someone nudge you to remind you about completing a task.

- To-do lists are always helpful. Have short deadlines and make the first task a small one. Quick and easy successes will encourage you.

- It's important to break a big task into smaller tasks which, when accomplished, will complete the big task. Small tasks make it all easier too.

- "What's the next step?" Should become your mantra.

- Take time on a frequent basis to review your progress, but it's best to complete these reviews without distractions, so turn off the television.

- Understand the reason for the task in the first place, and reward yourself when you accomplish it.

- If you're not happy in your job, and have no passion for it, then start looking for a job that provides you with what you want. Earning good money does not necessarily make you happy at work.

- Networking is an excellent way to find new opportunities.

- Friends, previous employers, professional groups and associations, and alumni associations are all places to start making contacts.

- On the web, LinkedIn is an excellent resource for professional contacts.

- Embrace professionalism at work. Be punctual, efficient, competent, and reliable.

- We live in an age where politeness stands out because society has become ruder and grosser. Being polite and courteous will get you noticed in a very positive way.

- Dress well. It's another way of being different from the crowd. We live in an age where it's okay to dress down for the office. Don't and you will be noticed in a very positive way. Good clothes are a solid investment.

Our financial life is provided through work. The money we earn makes our lifestyle possible. Make sure your financial house is in order so your lifestyle can provide you with the happiness and joy that will fulfill your life.

about the author

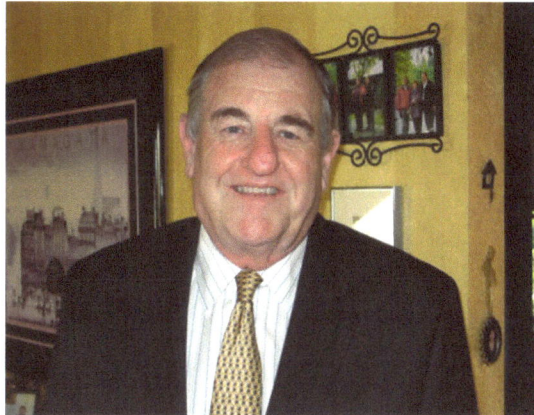

Donald Spillane

Born and educated in England, Don served with distinction as a "Bobbie" and a detective with Scotland Yard.

Now, he brings his extensive experience and knowledge from the business world to the table. From the newspaper, commercial real estate, financial services and computer software industries, Don has functioned as an owner, partner, director, senior manager and consultant for local, national and international companies.

He has co-founded start up companies, negotiated venture capital and uses a unique process to help both individuals and business owners achieve their personal, professional and financial priorities through his company, Designing Financial Solutions, Inc.

Don's real estate experience extends to ownership, management and negotiation of apartment buildings, retail shopping centers, industrial units and mobile home parks.

He is a published author and has been a contributing correspondent to a Japanese magazine about real estate in California. He has taught continuing education seminars approved by the Oregon Bar Association, the California Department of Real Estate and The Professionals In Human Resources (PIHRA) on subjects as diverse as long term care and commercial real estate. He also lectures to university students on financial subjects.

Don holds life insurance licenses for the States of California, Oregon and Washington and a real estate sales license for the State of California.

He lives in Los Angeles, California with his wife, Carol and their beagle, Lola Bea.

www.ingramcontent.com/pod-product-compliance
Lightning Source LLC
Chambersburg PA
CBHW041443210326
41599CB00004B/112